Before joining AMA in 1948, Lawrence A. Appley was vice president and director of Montgomery Ward and Company and of the Vick Chemical Company. During World War II he served as assistant to the Secretary of War and later as executive director and deputy chairman of the War Manpower Commission. He holds Doctor of Laws degrees from Ohio Wesleyan, St. Lawrence, and Colgate Universities, and from Bethany College. He is a trustee of Colgate University, Cazenovia College, and The Northfield Schools, and a director of the Harris-Intertype Corporation, The Standard Oil Company (Ohio), the Sheraton Corporation of America, the Stouffer Foods Corporation, the National Biscuit Company, the Brunswick Corporation, the Glen Ridge (New Jersey) Trust Company, the Dayco Corporation, and the General Time Corporation.

Mr. Appley is the author of *Management in Action*, published in 1956 and now in its fifth printing. Both *Management in Action* and this new collection of his writings draw on "The President's Scratchpad," Mr. Appley's monthly column in AMA's MANAGEMENT NEWS.

THE MANAGEMENT EVOLUTION

About This Book and Its Author

Lawrence A. Appley became president of the American Management Association in July 1948. Since that time, he has been identified in a very personal way with every phase of the Association's activity. In particular, through "The President's Scratchpad" in AMA's MANAGEMENT NEWS, his brief and pungent commentaries on managers, their problems, responsibilities, and opportunities have become familiar to an ever-widening audience of AMA members and friends. Mr. Appley's much-read *Management in Action* drew on the "Scratchpads" published in MANAGEMENT NEWS during his first years as president; it might have been predicted, as happened, that the demand for the book would immediately exhaust the first printing in the spring of 1956 and eventually require three more. This new collection of subsequent "Scratchpads" marks the completion of Mr. Appley's fifteenth year of AMA service.

THE MANAGEMENT EVOLUTION

By LAWRENCE A. APPLEY

AMERICAN MANAGEMENT ASSOCIATION

Library of Congress catalog card number: 63:14147

To one of the greatest of the professions—MANAGEMENT.

Foreword

THE MANY WHO HAVE HAD THE PRIVILEGE of knowing Lawrence A. Appley personally, or who have been inspired by the message he has made his life's work, not only credit him with ability, industry, and character but respect and honor him for his unremitting efforts to raise the level of managerial competence and to enlighten people generally about the vital importance of sound management in this highly competitive era.

This book carries Mr. Appley's good work to further heights. Anyone desirous of improving his performance as a manager in these difficult times will profit by a careful study of its contents. It will fortify his courage.

In the past decade, management has made great strides toward true professionalism. Not only are today's executives increasingly aware of the nature of their jobs, but there is growing realization among them of the complex environment in which they live and in which they must operate. The manager who is in fact a competent administrator recognizes that technical know-how, regardless of how well developed it may be, is in itself insufficient. Knowledge of people and what makes them tick must be merged with it.

Getting things done through people—and done properly—is the real test. Human hearts, souls, and minds must be won by the modern employer. As valuable as these are, they cannot be bought. The loyalty of the company's workforce is something that management must earn.

These are just a few of the basic truths to be gleaned from a reading of the pages which follow. Obviously, time and space prevent mentioning them all here. Throughout the book, however, the author advises us to—

- Think big.
- Set our sights on the future.
- Plan carefully.
- Keep faith with our fellow man.
- Act decisively.

I commend this book to the reader. I commend its author for his further contribution to that greater managerial effectiveness which is more than ever essential to our nation's welfare.

Clarence Francis

Contents

Introduction: Management the Simple Way

ONCE I WROTE A BOOK THAT FOLLOWED ALL the rules: It had an impressive, all-inclusive title; it had a preface, an introduction, an index; it contained research references, appendix and bibliography; and between its covers were the findings of some 15 years' experience with staff and line executives, top and middle management, supervisors, foremen and lead men.

The book suffered, however, from at least one common weakness—it made a simple, natural process appear complicated and difficult. The result was that many of those who might have profited by it did not finish it, while those who did finish it were too confounded by the apparent complexity of the subject to act on many of the recommendations.

Is it not odd how men and women like to complicate and distort simple, natural activities? Why do we fight

EDITORIAL NOTE: This discussion of management's essential simplicity was included in the author's *Management in Action*, published in 1956. Because he still looks upon it as a particularly apt statement of his management philosophy, he has requested that it be reprinted here.

the obvious? Why do we insist upon flying in the face of facts and principles which have been tested and proved over the years? Why do we continue to insist that we are different, that the people with whom we deal are different, that the activities in which we are engaged and the problems with which we are faced are different? Why do we continue to demand special consideration and tailor-made treatment? All we accomplish is to make things difficult for ourselves and unpleasant for those around us.

No automobile is exactly the same as another. Most automobiles look different; they have varied origins; they operate in multiple environments, perform numerous functions, and are used in many geographic areas and under normal and extreme climatic conditions. But they all work on the same principles: Their engines will stop without fuel; their parts will break down without proper care; their tires will go flat if punctured; they will skid without chains. No one of them will perform in the same way for different drivers, and no two of them respond alike for the same driver. Sailboats are like that too. So are people. *They all operate according to the same basic principles, and all have individual personalities.*

We think of the Gettysburg Address as a masterpiece of simplicity, but there is a much older pronouncement which by comparison makes the Gettysburg Address look like a Federal income tax statement. The modernized version is, "Do unto others as you would have them do unto you."

There, in one sentence, is the greatest book ever written, on the greatest subject there is, by the greatest author that ever lived. There is the main principle of good management in its simplest form. Why do we need more? Why do we require tons of books to explain something so simple?

It can only be because of our stubborn human desire to write the rules our own way. "Do unto others what we think ought to be done." That version of the rule opens the door to all our selfish motives. It warps our judgments, creates economic depressions, gives rise to pressure groups, loses wars. It causes us to hold tenaciously to pet prejudices, outworn traditions, antiquated practices, and valueless, time-consuming procedures. It creates duplication of effort, induces neglect of responsibilities, fosters misunderstandings and jealousies, and makes for friction and lost time. In other words, it makes a simple job difficult. *When prejudice and selfishness enter, reason, justice and simplicity exit.*

There has been so much written about "executive abilities," "administrative talents," and "managerial qualifications," and there have been so many arguments about whether leaders are born or made, that the whole field of leadership has been engulfed in mysticism. As a result, many actual and potential managers develop fear complexes and imagine complicated situations where none exist.

The truth of the matter is that leadership is a perfectly natural status in life. The world divides itself casually into leaders and followers. In any situation, such a division takes place, and no one can stop it. Civilization is bound to progress (assuming you have any faith in a Supreme Plan for the universe), and progress depends upon leadership. The process of natural selection, therefore, will generally provide good leaders.

The situation is complicated somewhat, however, because some of us feel that the whole future of the world depends upon us—that if we do not bring about perfection during our regimes the world is doomed. If we would only stop to realize that competent people contributed to world progress long before our time and that there are capable people still to be born, we should be more sympathetic toward the idea of leaving something for posterity to do.

Let us each make his own contribution with as little fuss and feathers as possible and in a simple and natural way. This does not mean we should work any less hard, but it does mean that there is little merit in being busy just for the sake of being busy. *Activity is of value only in terms of attainment.*

It would seem that we should be convinced by now that the success of any organization depends on having an adequate number of human beings in the right jobs at the right time, all producing at their highest capacity —outstanding people have told us so often enough. Then why do many of us expect intelligent human relations to develop spontaneously, while most of our time and effort is devoted to consideration of production schedules, transportation facilities, availability of raw materials, prices and markets?

It complicates management activity to a great degree when a struggle is necessary to place personnel activities on the same level of importance in the minds of operating officials as material items. Whenever consideration of the human element has a place other than of primary importance in management circles, ultimate success of the organization is made more difficult.

Management has been defined in very simple terms as "*getting things done through the efforts of other people*," and that function breaks down into at least two major responsibilities, one of which is *planning*, the other *control*.

Planning encompasses the whole field of deciding what you want human beings to accomplish. This involves the careful determination of needs, the establishment of objectives, the outlining of procedures that will attain those objectives, and the proper assignment of responsibility to individuals or groups of individuals.

If it is impossible to build a house without a blueprint, without some indication of what the carpenters, electricians, masons, plumbers and painters are to do, how can we expect to manufacture a product or render a service without the same careful planning?

Control requires the use of various media which will impel the people in the organization to work in accordance with the plan. There are at least two control factors that require careful attention: One is *organization structure,* and the other is *supervision.*

Unless the *organization structure* is simple and unless all who are part of it understand it, it will defeat its own purpose, which is to enable people to work together in groups as effectively as they would work alone. If there is misunderstanding about individual and/or departmental authority and responsibility, or about interrelationships between individuals and organization units, people cannot work effectively.

The function of *supervision* is to close the gaps between desired performance and actual human performance. If the mere issuance of policies and instructions would induce people to do what they are supposed to do, supervision would not be necessary.

Having divided the activity of management into the two basic elements of planning and control, it is simple to arrive at a statement of the *primary executive function—to determine what you want people to accomplish, to check periodically on how well they are accomplishing it, to find and train people competent for such accomplishment, to see that methods are developed by which they will perform more effectively, and to discipline them.*

This all leads us to a rather simple truth: *Management is the development of people and not the direction of things.* If this fact were more generally accepted, many management difficulties would disappear. The executive or supervisor who says that he would rather exhaust himself doing things correctly than expend the time and patience necessary to get other people to do them correctly is admitting that he cannot manage.

From these deductions it is not difficult to comprehend the fact that management and personnel administration are one and the same. They should never be separated. *Management is personnel administration.*

Since management requires staff and line activities, it is natural to divide personnel functions between staff and line executives, providing one appreciates the significance of each. *Line executives have complete and final responsibility for personnel matters and final authority for them. Staff personnel executives are expected to advise, help, and be of service to the line in the fulfilment of these responsibilities.* There is an important place for both in any administrative setup.

What complicates an otherwise simple matter is the desire on the part of some operating executives to delegate all personnel responsibility to a staff personnel executive and/or department as well as the desire on the part of some personnel executives to seize such responsibility. If this is permitted, the human element cannot receive proper consideration.

Consumer acceptance of products or services is dependent upon public good will—that is a well-accepted truism. It is also axiomatic that public good will is influenced the most by the employees of the organization—those who are selling the products or rendering the services. *Good employee relations within an organization are, therefore, the most important contributing factor to a sound and successful business.*

If you are to build sound employee relations, your dealings with the human beings in your organization must take into account the perfectly natural, simple motives and desires of those human beings. To clarify that point, let us consider a few of these natural interests. As they are presented, think of yourself as the employee. If you agree that they apply to you personally, you can rest assured that they apply to every worker under your direction.

1. *When an individual is seeking a new connection, he likes to be treated courteously and made to feel at home and at ease.* Under such conditions, he can be natural and show himself to the best advantage. That means that the individual seeking a job does not like to be herded down some back alley into a drab cell of an employment office. And when he arrives there, he does not like to be treated like a criminal in the line-up at police headquarters. The prospective employee's contact with the employment office is his first impression of the organization for which he may be working in a few days. In the atmosphere of an employment office, you sow the first seeds of morale.

2. *The average individual likes to be welcomed to a job rather than thrown into it.* Without much effort, simple induction procedures and orientation training can be provided. Such a program makes the new employee feel that he is considered an entity of some value, not a non-productive nuisance. The average person does not like to be shoved at an unsympathetic foreman, who in turn hands him over to some skilled

mechanic to whom a greenhorn is a pest. Yet new workers are receiving such treatment every day.

3. *The ordinary human being would like to receive simple and intelligent instruction in what he is expected to do, how it can be done, and what constitutes a job well done.* A simple program of job instruction which will enable the new employee to master his own job and prepare himself for a better one is not hard to devise. Agreement on what constitutes a job well done can be brought about by the establishment of simple standards of performance, in terms of quantity, quality, time, cost, and tests to be met. Working without standards is like participating in an athletic contest without any system of scoring.

4. *Any human being likes to work under someone whom he can respect and in whom he can have confidence.* The greatest single morale-builder is the feeling on the part of a worker, "I like to work for that man." To foster that feeling, capable supervision is necessary. But intelligent, capable supervision can be developed only through a management-planned and -administered program of continuous supervisory training. This also is a simple practice which pays big dividends.

5. *Every individual likes someone to recognize his or her importance.* One of the simple driving motives in human nature is the desire to have a place in the sun. A management which recognizes that each individual on the payroll has some intelligence, some ability, and something to contribute to the company's

policies and operations—no matter how small the contribution may be—has satisfied a basic desire. Human beings like to be heard, and they like to have their opinions and suggestions considered and respected. Channels of communication between top management and employees will, if established and kept open, contribute toward this end. Conferences, personal contacts between bosses and employees, suggestion systems, house organs, and the like are all simple methods of establishing such channels. Intelligent grievance procedure, which gives any employee the right to reach top management, is essential.

6. *Many human beings like to feel their daily work is of service to others.* In fact, the greater the opportunity for service, and the more the employee realizes it, the less the demand for material recognition. Knowledge of the organization involved—its objectives, policies, accomplishments, management philosophy, and the part each worker plays in them—all help to satisfy this natural human desire.

7. *There are few human beings who do not desire realistic recognition of a job well done.* We all like to be paid what the work we do is worth, and in accordance with employer capacity to pay. We all like to receive promotions when our abilities and merits justify them. Simple systems of job evaluation, salary and wage administration, merit rating and job progression would satisfy this desire. Why are they not in greater use?

8. *There are few human beings who will not work*

hard and long for incentive. Special recognition always inspires greater effort. A pat on the back has its merits, but a medal on the uniform is tangible evidence of management appreciation. Special awards, bonuses, prizes, etc., fairly administered, increase human desire to produce. Why do we try to complicate such simple things as incentives? Why do we try to level off rewards, to treat everyone alike, regardless of attainment? Why do we do so when we know that a simple human impulse is to produce more when more recognition is possible?

9. *Every human being likes to work in an organization in which there is universal confidence in the ability and fairness of top management.* Most people who are worth their salt will go through hell for a leader in whom they believe. They will put up with anything because of their confidence in him. A management which is frank and above-board, which has in it no vestige of paternalism, which is fair and open in its business and labor negotiations, will satisfy this inherent desire. Management reports to employees, personal contacts during which management and employees come to know each other as personalities, are simple means to this end.

10. *All of us want to be sound of mind and body.* Consequently it helps when others take an interest in our health, and particularly when our bosses do—we cannot work well when mentally or physically ill. Vacations with pay, medical examinations and services, hospitalization plans, safety programs, credit

unions, employee counseling, all help the employee to keep well. Incidentally, they will pay dividends in increased production and improved morale.

11. A *basic instinct in all of us is the desire for security.* When a human being is worried about his job or about the welfare of those dependent on him, he cannot produce effectively. We all know that our earning capacity is certain to diminish eventually, and the fear of want in old age is constantly before us. Annuity plans, insurance programs, opportunities for savings, job stability, all help to counteract this fear. And they are all possible if we but have the will to create them.

12. *When it is necessary for an employee to terminate relations with an employer, he likes to do so with his head in the air and with a full understanding of the reasons for termination.* He does not like to be notified of his termination by a pink slip attached to his time card. If termination is for cause, he does not like some mushy-mouthed, smooth-acting diplomat to lie to him. A properly conducted and timed exit interview would, in most cases, satisfy his normal wish to know the facts.

These, then, are some simple truths about human beings. Added up, they make plain, everyday horse sense. Why, then, do we tend to make them needlessly complicated?

If one were to summarize all the different ways of insuring good management that have been suggested over the years, the list would run into the hundreds. But it would be of little value because the average operating executive or supervisor would probably take one look at it and decide that the whole matter was too complicated to act upon in one short lifetime.

In the interest of simplicity, a few steps are outlined at this point. If followed carefully and with reasonable attention to sequence, they will insure adequate management attention to the way in which operations are conducted. With both old and new employees and in both old and new situations, application of these recommendations will bring about improvement in human performance.

1. (With the person involved) *Develop a simple outline of the functions and operations to be performed.* This can apply to an individual job or to any complete unit of an organization. It should include an understandable statement of what people are to do, what authority they have in doing it, and what their relationships with other people are.

2. (With the person involved) *Develop a simple statement of results which will be considered satisfactory.* There are many activities for which, at first, it seems impossible to develop standards of performance. However, discussion of them in a sincere attempt to develop standards will often produce very definite and acceptable objectives.

3. (With the person involved) *At regular intervals, check actual performance against the standards that have been set.* If management is to plan its activities, it must know how big a gap there is between what is being done and what should be done. This should be

checked in terms of individual and group attainment.

4. (With the person involved) *Make a list of corrective actions necessary to improve performance where such improvement is needed.* An individual cannot develop into a better worker and a better citizen unless he is continuously increasing his skill, gaining knowledge, changing his habits, and assuming constructive attitudes. A manager should know where improvement is needed.

5. (With the person involved) *Select the best sources from which he can obtain help and information.* Sources can be divided into four categories: the immediate supervisor, other individuals in the organization, people outside the organization who could be brought in, and outside sources of help to which the individuals concerned could be referred. These sources should be considered in that order, and the one which is the most advantageous selected.

6. (With the person involved) *A time should be set aside in advance for supplying the help and information that is needed.* If we do not plan in advance, the time can be made available only through disrupting the functioning of the organization. It is of little use to go to all the trouble of deciding what should be done, analyzing what has been done, and determining what action is needed, if no action is taken.

7. (With the person involved) *Arrive at mutual agreement as to what constitutes a fair day's pay for a fair day's work, as well as what non-financial incentives are worth working for.* On a firm base of fairly ad-

ministered financial rewards, a climate can be developed that will cause people to stay with you rather than go elsewhere for more money.

No specific system of carrying out these recommendations is needed. *Method* is relatively unimportant if a continuous attempt is made by intelligent people to do what is suggested.

It seems a simple and natural conclusion that the people in the organization should receive as much attention as material items. If this were done in a conscious, orderly way rather than in haphazard and spasmodic bursts of enthusiasm, the results would be astounding.

It is an interesting commentary on human nature that many of us must see a new project spelled out in detail before we attempt it. We then argue about the details and sometimes refuse to take action because we cannot see how to cross every bridge in advance. If those in positions of responsibility would determine the fundamental "rightness" of a proposition and then with unshakable faith in that judgment move on to find the way, human progress would be more rapid than it is now. There is so much argument about methods and techniques that the question of basic "rightness" or "wrongness" is sometimes overlooked.

Perfection in any activity can be attained only through practice. If no one had been willing to fly the original airplane because it was not a perfect mechanism, where would air transportation be today? What we are flying today is probably not nearly so good as the planes 10 years from now will be. The same is true of management methods of dealing with the human element.

It is said of General Pershing that during World War I when one of the members of his staff complained that a certain officer at the front was making many mistakes, his reaction was, "That's right, but he's making them fast." He who makes no mistakes makes no progress. He who makes progress without mistakes is not human.

If what is outlined here seems reasonable and sound and if we have faith enough in it to make a start on some of those things from which we have shied away, we are in for some pleasant management experiences. A human being reacts quickly and favorably to understanding, fairness and consideration. If we approach our management activities with the idea of doing things in the simple, natural way, much of the confusion and frustration which we now experience will disappear.

The greatest single reward which any manager, supervisor, foreman or lead man can receive is to have those who have been under his direction say that they are better workers, better citizens, and better producers because of his leadership. Such an attitude builds morale and loyalty, and these will accomplish the impossible.

PART ONE

Management as a Profession

The man at the wheel may be replaced, may be put under a new authority, may be regarded differently by the crew, and may work with different instruments in a different way, but the functions performed remain constant, essential under every conceivable circumstance. It is important, therefore, that we should devise a philosophy of management, a code of principles, scientifically determined and generally accepted, to act as a guide, by reason of its foundation upon ultimate things, for the daily practice of the profession.

Oliver Sheldon
The Philosophy of Management

Ten Commandments of Management

Few professions, sciences, or arts have so great a body of knowledge as has management. Few bodies of knowledge have had so many contributors over so long a period of time. Less has been done in management, however, than in many other professions to identify, codify, and make appropriate knowledge and experience available.

It is most gratifying to see the intense interest that is now developing and the activity that is being organized to put management know-how into ready and usable form for those who need and want it. Probably never in all history has so much effort been spent at one time to put knowledge in acceptable form as is now being exerted in the field of management. Our universities and colleges, management consultants, professional societies, and management practitioners are increasing their efforts and expenditures so rapidly that it is almost impossible to keep track of everything that is going on.

It is estimated that more than half a million executives take part in formal educational and training programs in the course of a calendar year. Such extensive application to management improvement requires accompanying research, study, and analysis in the preparation of materials and the reporting of proceedings. The size of it all is staggering and at the same time inspiring.

People frequently ask what some of the most significant principles and truths are that have emerged from all this. Any individual who seeks to reply must do so in terms of his own thinking and evaluation. I am taking the liberty of setting down my own answer to this question. That answer has changed and will change from year to year, but, as of the moment, the following seem to me to be the ten most important commandments for people who are engaged in leadership responsibilities:

1. Identify the people of an organization as its greatest asset.
2. Make profit in order to continue rendering service.
3. Approach every task in an organized, conscious manner so that the outcome will not be left to chance.
4. Establish definite long- and short-range objectives to insure greater accomplishment.
5. Secure full attainment of objectives through general understanding and acceptance of them by others.

6. Keep individual members of the team well adjusted by seeing that each one knows what he is supposed to do, how well he is supposed to do it, what his authority is, and what his work relationships with others should be.
7. Concentrate on individual improvement through regular review of performance and potential.
8. Provide opportunity for assistance and guidance in self-development as a fundamental of institutional growth.
9. Maintain adequate and timely incentives and rewards for increase in human effort.
10. Supply work satisfactions for those who perform the work and those who are served by it.

It is interesting to note that all but two of these commandments directly affect human beings. It never fails. Whenever people get together to discuss management, to talk about leadership, to review their most serious problems and their most successful attainments, they spend most of the time talking about people and human relationships.

The original Ten Commandments have proved over the centuries to be sound guidance for individual conduct. Individual conduct has significance principally when related to life with others. Management is unquestionably a matter of individual conduct as a basis for inspiring the finest of thinking and practice on the part of other people.

An individual manager is not necessarily a model of perfect leadership capability because he thinks of human beings as the most important factor in an organization. No manager, however, can be adequate without such a belief. While many people in management state proudly that they are not in business primarily for profit, they will not continue to render the service for which they are in business unless they do make a profit.

Many jobs are completed successfully even though they are done in a haphazard, hit-or-miss, rule-of-thumb manner. But no job is done as well as it could have been if a little more conscious effort and order had been introduced into the approach. While many executives make progress without knowing exactly where they are going, there is no manager who would not make much more progress if his objectives were long-range and specific.

People will do things without understanding what or why, and many follow requests and instructions blindly. All people, however, will work harder when they understand and accept what it is they are trying to accomplish. Any individual is happier in his work situation when there is complete understanding between him and his boss as to what he is supposed to do and what his relationships are with others in doing it.

The performance of individuals should and must be reviewed by their leaders and discussed with the individuals involved. The purpose of such review, however, should be to point out opportunities for improvement and for advancement. When someone feels that he is being given all possible assistance, guidance, and opportunity to perform to his very best, he has the fundamentals for the highest type of morale.

Surely no leader will disagree that greater effort and better results justify appropriate rewards. Rewards, however, are both financial and non-financial, and some of the greatest of the latter arise out of work relationships and accomplishment. When those who are served and those who are rendering service have a full sense of satisfaction in what has been done, the perpetuation of the organization and of the leadership that brought about those results is assured.

The Management Factor

THE MANAGEMENT FACTOR IS THE IMPACT OF positive managerial action upon the course of events. It is the activation of pre-determined means toward the attainment of pre-established goals.

The management factor is the "something" a manager does to produce different results from those to be expected if events are left to follow their own course. It is what happens when a manager "does something about it."

Leroy Lattin, president of the General Telephone Company of California, has a quaint way of drawing attention to long-established admonishments which are known so well that we overlook their lessons. He makes them so ridiculous that they attract immediate attention and then register correctly with full force. One of his favorites is: "Don't do something, stand there!"

If a retail store has doubled its business in ten years merely by opening its doors each morning, what would it have done if the owner did something about it? If known population trends into the future insure a utility company a steady increase in volume of consumer demand, how much more might be expected if management expended effort to step up the pace of progress?

When competition threatens the survival of a company, destruction is assured if worry is the only defense. The positive action taken to stop or slow down competitive inroads represents the management factor.

The establishing of a long-term objective does not insure its attainment. A forecast is not a statement of what is going to happen. A projection of past results into the future does not portray the future. Something has to be done about it.

The management factor in a manager—sensitivity to his own power to influence people and events—usually expresses itself through a conscious evolution:

1. Clear *identification of a need* for change.
2. Development of an idea or alternative ideas of *what will fill the need.*
3. Transmission of need and *idea to the minds of others.*
4. Determination of the best *program to activate the idea.*
5. Testing the *economics.*
6. *Selection of the person* or persons qualified to carry out the idea.

While outlining this sequence, there is vividly in my mind a specific illustration. Two years ago, the president of a well-established company in a stable, basic industry decided that management's concept of the future should not be merely a projection of the past. He saw the need to do something about it.

After considerable deliberation and study, he acquired what became a firmly held idea that formal long-range planning was indicated as it never had been done in the company before. After weighing alternatives in consultation with others, he set his mind firmly in the direction of expertly planning the future rather than leaving its development to chance.

This president then set about transmitting his thinking into the minds of the other top executives. During the next six months, fourteen full days were devoted to actual long-range planning by top management as a group, with the president participating at all times, and ten days to discussion between individuals. (Effective transmission of thought with essential motivation is not always a short process.) After this group developed broad but specific goals, the kind of program needed was determined.

It was decided that expert staff assistance was necessary to do an adequate long-range-planning job. The top operating group could not give the time required for the extensive and vital staff work indicated. The economics of the situation seemed sound and practical.

A position specification was drawn up for a vice president for management planning. The organization was thoroughly screened for talent that might be made available. There being none, a man was employed from outside.

Four months later, I heard the VP for planning

make his first formal presentation to the management. It was magnificent! Here was a man who knew what he was doing and was doing it well. Long-range planning is now in that company to stay, and the company will be better for it.

A need was identified; an idea to meet it was formed; the idea was transmitted to those involved; a program was formulated; the economics indicated its soundness; a qualified man was selected; the idea is now a reality; and a need is being met. Something was done about it. This is one factor that makes a man a manager.

Indices of Good Management

HOW CAN ONE TELL WHETHER A BUSINESS—one's own company, a subsidiary, a division, or a firm being considered for acquisition or merger—is being well managed? What are the indices of a scientifically managed business?

To pinpoint these questions a bit more—how does one know a good manager when he sees him? What are the indices of the professional manager?

There is a tendency to oversimplify the answers to these questions. In reply to the question, "How do you know a good manager?" the quick response is likely to be, "Look at the balance sheet. Is he making a satisfactory profit?" But it isn't quite that easy.

There are managements and managers who are making high profits but ruining the business. It does not require a tremendous amount of ability to milk a going concern of all the profits to be wrung out of it and then turn the emaciated carcass over to someone else to liquidate.

Here are a few of the basic evidences, presented in terms of executive actions rather than personal qualities. These indices are not intended as an all-inclusive list. They are simply some bench marks, any one of which can suggest many more:

1. A reasonable period of good profit performance. (This is subject to interpretation in terms of the specific situation.)
2. A one-year operating budget.
3. Individual departmental programs supporting budget figures.
4. A one-year capital expenditure budget.
5. A quarterly estimate of deviations from budgets with indications of action being taken.
6. A long-range (at least five to ten years) product development and distribution plan in visual form.
7. A written forecast of conditions (economic, industry, labor, material, etc.) under which objectives must be attained.
8. A manual containing the major company policies under the headings of "General," "Personnel," "Manufacturing," "Marketing," etc.
9. Written descriptions for all management jobs.
10. An organization chart, not more than one year old, showing relationships among all positions.
11. A formal personnel development program (for both management and non-management people).
12. A reports system for supplying vital information at all levels.

13. Regular staff meetings for performance review.
14. Good housekeeping!

The existence of such practices in an organization does not insure good management. However, their existence does insure better management than the organization would have without them, and good management of the future will require them.

These indices are applicable not to top management alone but also, with some modifications, to all management levels. While some managers produce no income and are in a position simply to control expense, all managers make some contribution to profit and should identify that contribution. While some managers do not establish long-range plans for the company, do the forecasting, or set major policies, all managers contribute to these activities and should be conscious of them. All these indices of good management mark the good manager, be he foreman, supervisor, department head, or officer.

There are distinct differences between the professional golfer, the self-trained weekender, and the dub. Believe me, these differences are becoming more marked in management with each passing year.

What Else!

ON NUMEROUS OCCASIONS ONE HEARS A STATEment made by a business executive that sounds something like this: "By the use of sound management principles and the selection of competent personnel, we were able to get the job done." Just recently I heard a speaker say this three or four times during an address on how to operate in foreign lands. His firm had been phenomenally successful over a relatively short period of time in getting started abroad.

This is one of those phrases which, because we hear them frequently, lose their significance. On the other hand, what an impact it has all in itself—"sound management principles and competent personnel." What else! What else is required for the attainment of a given objective? This combination of words is actually an extremely brief summary of a long list of elements essential for successful performance of any executive task.

Think for a moment what the phrase "sound management principles" encompasses. If the most experienced manager in the world were to spend a solid month doing nothing but listing all the sound management principles he could put down, he still would be a long way from covering them all. They would have to comprise the whole activity of leadership from planning to attainment.

When one hears "sound management principles" and gives the matter any thought, certain ideas pass through his mind. Here are a few of them: setting basic objectives; establishing short- and long-range plans; developing basic policies; setting performance standards; building organization structure, including describing positions, delegating authority, and clarifying relationships; maintaining communication; maintaining controls, inspection, and bases for continuing measurement; determining and decentralizing decision points; providing for timely and appropriate action; etc.

Here in one phrase—"sound management"—is a whole profession; an expertness; a wealth of experience and know-how; a background of technical information, skill, and training. By using "sound management principles" one can do almost anything provided he has the next ingredient—"competent personnel."

Consider, if you will, what is brought to the heart and mind of a responsible leader by that phrase—"competent personnel." This phrase means vital human beings with aptitudes to do the job at hand, with the skills, knowledge, habits, and attitudes needed to work enthusiastically and successfully.

When one thinks of a competent person, he visualizes a whole galaxy of sound personnel practices required to obtain, hold, and motivate him or her: the discovery of good sources of the competency desired; adequate interviewing, testing, and employment; proper orientation to the company and the job, including training for the job; adequate and fair pay, incentives, and other types of financial rewards; careful training on the job and for bigger jobs; adequate appraisal and review; appropriate non-financial incentives; suitable fringe benefits; proper methods of motivation; a good climate and work environment; effective selection and development of the top management team, including provision for reserves in depth; thorough preparation for first-line supervision; etc.; etc.

In other words, two simple expressions encompass all the requirements of a management job well done. If an executive has good, competent, willing people and follows sound management principles and practices, how can he fail? What else is required?

While repetition is effective in transferring thought to the minds of others, it can also make people so accustomed to hearing something again and again that the significance of the thought is dulled. When, therefore, we hear "sound management principles and competent personnel," let us give thought to all of the time, the work, the effort, the know-how, the skill, and the patience that go into the realization of such a condition.

Management of Labor, Agriculture, and Government

FREQUENTLY ONE SEES THE PHRASE "MANAGEMENT, labor, agriculture, and government." In fact, it appears so often as to lead one to believe that full comprehension of what management really is does not exist on a broad scale. There seems to be an impression that management is a class, a group, an entity.

Management is an activity that is involved in the life of every individual and in every group of individuals. Instead of speaking of management, labor, agriculture, and government, we should refer to business management, industrial management, labor management, agricultural management, and governmental management.

Organized labor has both managerial and operating activities. A farm requires both farm management and actual farming. Any government agency has its workers and its managers. Every individual has management problems in directing his own life and activities. Management is not a class. It is a type of work, and it exists wherever there is work.

One often hears the proposition that labor, agriculture, and management should be represented in government. (You can add to these any other groups into which human beings are divided, such as educational and religious.) But management as such cannot be represented. Management represents the particular group that it manages. Labor is represented by its management. Agriculture is represented by its management. That is one of the functions of management. Industrial and business management doesn't represent management; it represents business and industry.

Business and industry happen to be the group that pays the most attention to the qualifications, selection, training, and performance of managers. No other group with which I am acquainted gives so much recognition and thought to management as a part of its over-all functioning. Government has identified and focused some attention upon the function of public administration, but no government has given the recognition or taken the action required to guarantee competent management and/or administration.

It is interesting to note that other groups are beginning to show some awareness of the importance of management. Some persons are beginning to acknowledge that there is a factor in the running of a hospital other than medicine, surgery, nursing, feeding, and housing. It is hospital management. A few of our universities now are teaching hospital administration.

Courses in educational administration are being developed to a greater degree than ever before. Educators are beginning to admit that the management of an educational institution is a specific function in addition to the development of an academic curriculum and the teaching. Some of our universities and colleges actually look for managers rather than educators to administer their institutions—although a manager *and* educator is ideal if he can be found.

Murmurings about farm management—farm administration—are beginning to be heard. In a matter of time it will be commonly acknowledged that farmers must be trained in farm management as well as in farming. That time may be a long way off, but at least there are hopeful signs.

Organized labor is recognizing that it has management problems much the same as those of corporations; there is a good deal of interest in organized labor circles in the study of management as such within unions.

All this adds up to the following observation: When looking for a manager, make management the basis of selection rather than the group from which the individual comes. If a government agency, for example, is seeking a good administrator, it should look first within the government; then, if no such experienced government administrator is available, it should look elsewhere.

A business man should not be and usually is not appointed to an administrative post in government because he is a business man. He is appointed because he is a good, experienced manager with a record of successful accomplishment. No deliberate attempt should be made to pick a man for an administrative position because he is a labor man, a farmer, a preacher, a veteran, an industrialist, or an Indian. We should pick a manager. The group within which he has managed is of secondary importance.

Because business and industry have placed the greatest emphasis upon management, its qualifications, and its development, they are the source to which most other groups turn. We find business men going into government, into university administration, into hospital management, into non-profit and charitable organizations, and even into agriculture—not only because business is the best known source of managers but because it has a larger number of them than any other group.

Let us, therefore, be careful about identifying management as a particular class or group because management is an inherent part of every group. The sooner each group acknowledges this fact and does something about the effectiveness of its management, the more effective will the organization itself become, whether it be industry, labor, agriculture, or government.

PART TWO

The Manager as a Professional

I hold every man a debtor to his profession; from the which as men of course do seek to receive countenance and profit, so ought they of duty to endeavor themselves, by way of amends, to be a help and ornament thereunto.

Sir Francis Bacon
Maxims of the Law

Positive Personality

POSITIVE PERSONALITY IS SYNONYMOUS WITH effective leadership. This characterizes the kind of person who always moves with directness of purpose and skill of attainment. In fact, a real test of positive personality is possession of a continuing sense of accomplishment.

Such a person is frequently quite annoying and even irritating to neutral or negative personalities, but that is part of the price of leadership. He who moves with purpose, confidence, and results attracts responsibility to himself, and he is automatically set apart from the multitude. The heavier the responsibility, the greater the price to be paid by the one who carries it.

A positive personality gets things done. He inspires action. His judgment determines whether he turns out to be a good or bad leader; but, right or wrong, a man of action is a leader.

Positive personalities are to be found in any area of work: business, industry, agriculture, government, politics, military service, education, religion, and the many professional services. They move with a determination and a precision which indicate quite clearly that they have a pattern of action which governs their work. Their mental and physical movements are related to various steps which, when each is done well, result in the success of the whole. Let us take a look at some of these as I see them.

1. *The positive personality makes clear-cut decisions as to exactly where he wants to go.* He has goals—long- and short-range. He has them either in writing or so clearly in mind he can put them in writing.

It is usually found that those who ultimately end up as leaders were quite analytical in the determination of the kind of work they wished to do in life. They did not just take the first attractive opportunity that came along and follow the path of least resistance.

A positive personality always has a goal in mind, even though that goal may change frequently. The day-to-day decisions are made in relation to this goal.

2. *The positive personality determines a course of action or alternative courses to attain the goal set.* He is a student of strategy and a master of procedure.

The finest example of this and training for it is in the age-old game of chess. One has to think many moves ahead and frequently change one's plans in accordance with the unanticipated moves of the opposition.

The attainment of a goal requires a definite plan of action even though this plan may be continually changing. When a pilot sets out from New York to London, he has a flight plan. Storms may force him to alter his course on the way, but he at least started with something which he alters, and this is quite different from working out a plan as he proceeds.

3. *The positive personality estimates the type and amount of resources required to attain a given objective.* He approximates or budgets in advance what quantity and quality he requires over long periods of time and at different periods of time. He is very conscious of the type of organization structure that will be needed, the kind of people who will perform various responsibilities within that structure, the physical facilities that are paramount to his task, the raw materials called for, and the finances without which he cannot exist. This is not just for large organizations—this starts with a single individual.

That individual who is entirely self-centered and excludes all others from his existence is anything but a positive personality. Therefore, he must be ruled out of this discussion. The individual about whom we are speaking cannot live a life unrelated to others. In everything he does he has to take into consideration people and his relation to them—whether or not they are on his payroll. There is no life, other than that of a hermit, that is not dependent upon people, materials, and finances.

4. *The positive personality establishes specific controls*—indicators of the way in which things are going—so that he always knows the relationship of progress to plan. He budgets his resources. He provides places of safekeeping for them when not in use. He establishes

standards for each task and periodic measurements of performance against these standards. He places authority at points where action can be taken quickly when measurements indicate action is required.

A positive personality runs a "tight, taut ship" with everything having a purpose and with each purpose having justification.

5. *The positive personality motivates human action.* He can inspire, lead, get people to do more than others can do, and get them to do more than they think they can do. He provides service motives to all his people as well as great human satisfactions out of work and work output.

The positive personality does not bring these things about by sheer strength of personality or by "pep injections" or other patent-medicine types of treatment. He does it in a conscious, orderly, professional way. This is not primarily a matter of sparkle, oratory, drive, or great personal attractiveness. It has been done effectively by quiet, non-vocal, self-denying persons.

The positive personality is simply a person who knows where he is going, how to get there, and how to get other people to help him in the process. Seldom does one find such a person looking for personal favors or personal recognition. He is one who rallies others in a common cause in which all individual persons benefit as the cause is realized. He is usually a person of deep convictions who has confidence in the cause himself.

There is no greater human power than that of a person with a purpose plus the skill to attain it. Both purpose and skill are acquirable. The establishment of purpose requires, first, a consciousness that life is a matter of making decisions. There are distinct learnable processes for determining alternatives, for gathering and weighing facts, and for timing. What a purpose is, and what the best ways are for determining which one to accept, are clear-cut and available items of information. Skills required for attaining purposes are also identifiable and can be developed within human beings.

An Enlightened Manager

QUITE FREQUENTLY AN EXECUTIVE IS DEscribed as being "enlightened," "progressive," or "modern." The implication is clear—there is a type of manager different from others and favorably so. What qualities in the man give him this distinction? Here is my answer to that question—an answer that certainly is not final. Its contribution may be mostly in the discussion it provokes.

An *enlightened manager has a philosophy* of management. He has thought it through, discussed it freely with others, written it out, and tried to live it. If it is an enlightened philosophy, it is not in conflict with that stated by Clarence Francis, retired chairman of the board of General Foods Corporation and recipient of the Henry Laurence Gantt Medal for industrial statesmanship:

> I believe the greatest assets of a business are its human assets and that their improvement is both a matter of material advantage as well as moral obligation. I believe, therefore, that employees must be treated as honorable individuals, justly rewarded, encouraged in their progress, fully in-

formed, properly assigned, and that their lives and work must be given meaning and dignity on and off the job.

An enlightened manager is professional in his approach to his job. He is a career man just as is a doctor, a lawyer, a teacher, an engineer. He understands that management is an activity in itself, requiring particular qualifications, preparation, skills, and tools.

An amateur gloats over his successes. A professional is concerned over his mistakes. He is willing to make the sacrifices required in time, money, and energy to become trained in his activities, to practice, and to keep up to date. He fully appreciates that education is a continuing process—for the proficient it never ends.

An enlightened manager is scientific. He appreciates that there is a great body of knowledge available from the work and experience of his predecessors in the profession. Out of all this know-how have come basic principles—truths that are of inestimable value. He yearns to master them and takes every possible opportunity to learn of them.

Being scientific in one's work means being orderly and thoughtful, following a plan rather than leaving matters to chance in hit-or-miss fashion. It means guiding the future rather than being guided by it. It means acting rather than reacting. A scientific executive makes things happen.

An enlightened manager is an artist. He is highly skilled in individual effectiveness with people. He is a deep and constructive force in the lives of others. His greatness is to be found in the opportunity and help he

A CASE FOR THE PROFESSIONAL MANAGER

That person who sets a goal and then goes about reaching it in an organized, orderly, and conscious way

will accomplish more

than

he who leaves the future to chance and each day to take care of itself.

That person who performs in an organized, orderly, and conscious way

will be more effective

if he is educated, trained, and skilled in philosophy, methods, and tools

than

he who acquires his know-how from exposure and experience alone.

The more thorough, careful, and specialized the education, training, and practice a person experiences,

THE MORE PROFESSIONAL HE BECOMES!

The professional:

Understands what he is doing and how to go about it;
Is a student of the available body of knowledge;
Practices faithfully and rigorously;
Makes what he does his career—a means of livelihood;
Is dedicated—his profession is his major reason for living, his means of serving others.

The professional:

Is an individual who is mentally and physically trained, emotionally mature, and psychologically adjusted to perform the job at hand; he is better than an amateur.

The amateur and the professional:

The amateur performs as a sideline—for the pro, it's the main chance!
The amateur performs for fun—the pro for a life work and livelihood!
The amateur learns what time permits—the pro what the job requires!
The amateur practices when he can—the pro because he must!
The amateur excels because no one shows up who is better —the pro because no less standard is acceptable!
The amateur can quit when he wishes—the pro only when he is done!
The amateur gloats over his successes—the pro worries over his mistakes!
The amateur takes the breaks as they come—the pro makes them!

gives others in their self-betterment, not in criticizing and tearing others down.

An artist at management can secure the participation of his people in the determination of long- and short-range objectives and methods for attaining them. He can secure their understanding and acceptance of his objectives and their fullest effort in working toward the accomplishment of those objectives. He can be friendly, fair, and human while being firm and resolute.

An enlightened manager is humble. He acknowledges the existence of a power greater than himself. He has faith in many fine influences that he or any other manager cannot explain or prove. A humble manager is a self-critical, soul-searching person who is conscious of the breadth and depth of his responsibilities and accepts the obligations that go with them.

Such a manager is not a one-man operator; he is the coach of a team. He realizes that while he may know more about more activities than anyone else in his organization, there is someone in his organization who knows more about any one activity than he does. While he cannot out-expert the specialists, he is able to integrate their viewpoints and activities.

The enlightened manager is not to be found just at the top of an organization. He exists at every level of management from that of chairman of the board to that of foreman, first-line supervisor, and group leader. Whatever his title, he is always a good operator. He always has high morale in his organization. He always enjoys the respect and confidence of his people. He's a pretty good guy to be around!

The Certification of Managers

IT WOULD SEEM THAT SIGNIFICANT ENOUGH authorities have declared it, and there are sufficient facts available to support it, for management to be accepted as a profession without further question. Two declarations, symbolic of many others, come from impressive enough sources for my own personal satisfaction. I refer to Dean Courtney C. Brown of the Graduate School of Business of Columbia University and to Ralph J. Cordiner, chairman of the board of General Electric Company.

Dean Brown, before an AMA Marketing Conference in 1957, stated: "Education for business has come of age. It is now seriously lodged in the educational programs of the nation, along with the other great professional studies of law, medicine, theology, and engineering."

Mr. Cordiner, in his book, *New Frontiers for Professional Managers*, writes: "When the professional manager at every echelon of the organization recognizes that each of us has some distinctive and individual contribution that he alone can make and cherishes it as his most deeply held belief about his fellow men, then he has found the clue to leadership in the American society."

The facts support the observation that management is today where the medical profession was when doctors declared that working in a drug store or helping a doctor in his office was not sufficient training to be a doctor. Managers in large numbers have said within the past decade that helping managers or being exposed to managers is not sufficient training for the professional manager.

Ten years ago, it was difficult to locate more than 10,000 executives throughout a calendar year attending formal management training courses in universities, in their own companies, or in professional societies. It is reasonably well estimated that during one recent year more than half a million practicing managers formally enrolled in management courses.

Whereas ten years ago you could note on the fingers of one hand the universities that provided courses for mature business executives, it would be very difficult today to find any college or university with a business school that is not providing such courses. There has been over the past decade a fabulous growth in the number and activities of professional management societies.

Since management *is* a profession and since it calls for the use of scientific techniques, certification of qualified managers is implied.

It will be a long time before any educational institution or professional society will be presumptuous enough to take upon itself the certification of a manager. It is already an established practice in many companies, however, that the management of that company certifies its managers by passing upon their competency. The certification of a manager by the management of an organization in which that manaager works, or is to work, will take much more formal and specific shape in the not too distant future.

It is extremely difficult to certify how good a manager is. He may be outstanding today, mediocre tomorrow, and quite inadequate next year. This is true, for example, of automobile drivers. A very good driver at one moment could at another moment be a poor one because of certain physical or mental developments within himself. It is possible, however, to certify that a person has completed certain training and passed certain tests without which he could not be a good manager or a good driver.

There is little uniformity of opinion as to what kind of training a manager must have and what tests he should pass in order to receive certification. That management which takes such certification and tests seriously, however, should have a specific list of qualities, knowledge, and skills which are to be measured and should provide specific training for the acquiring of them. The following is submitted as an illustration.

1. *Emotional stability, psychological adjustment to the work to be done, and basic management aptitudes.* These should be ascertained by a battery of established,

proven, and professionally recognized personnel tests administered by experts.

Emotional stability is a reflection of maturity. No manager can be considered fit without it. If there are any tests that can be considered valid, they can be found in this area. Much study and experimentation have gone into this subject for a half century at least.

If a person is not psychologically adjusted to the work of a manager, nothing good can come of it. Many excellent individual producers, who have never wanted to be anything else, have been converted into failures as managers. The crippling belief that no person should earn more than his boss means that a specialist must become a manager in order to make more money. The athletic coach or manager certainly has exploded this myth because he is perfectly happy to have stars on his team making more than he is. For one thing, they are largely responsible for the size of his own income and, for another, they will not make these higher incomes for as long a period of time as the boss.

The basic management aptitudes are well known. They are the ability to think clearly; to plan precisely; to communicate effectively; to attract participation by others; to be decisive; to inspire. These are a few, the presence of which can be easily ascertained.

The time has come to acknowledge certain facts about personnel tests. They have had a long, hard road. There are today professional, validated, effective tests available for certain specific purposes. They should not be administered or interpreted, however, by anyone other than experts in personnel testing. For the results of a psychological or aptitude test to be given to a layman for interpretation is just as ridiculous as handing a patient the medical report of a doctor. These are not matters for amateurs, but have been proven in the hands of professionals.

A real test of the sincerity and dedication of a manager or a prospective manager is the extent of his willingness to submit to personnel testing. If he will not do so, this, in itself, is a significant signal.

2. *Personal qualifications.* They can be determined by actual observation or by providing test situations in which their presence will be established or found absent.

Probably more has been discussed and written on what constitutes the qualifications of an executive than on any other management subject. Usually, such a list ends in the description of an individual, only one of whom ever lived. It is interesting, however, to study the lists that have been provided on this subject and to notice those items which appear most frequently.

The following identification of desirable personal qualifications for a manager is not supposed to be all-inclusive or an end in itself; it is just illustrative. It assumes the presence of certain basic qualifications, without which a person should not even be on the payroll, such as honesty, loyalty, industry, intelligence, job knowledge, acceptable appearance, good personal habits, etc. The possession of any of the following qualifications of a manager is early ascertainable. Following each is a list of indicators:

A. *Sensitivity to detail.*

(1) Cleanliness, neatness, tidiness in person and work are found when this qualification is present. There is no excuse anywhere, even in a foundry, for a lack of these indicators. I have, myself, visited well-run plants where I would have been willing to eat off the machine shop floor—it was just that clean!

(2) Organization of self and work. This is obvious. The person who knows what he is doing and when he is going to do it and controls his activities so that he does what he has planned to do, rather than waiting for others to plan it for him, stands out.

(3) Promptness—concern for time. While it may seem picayune, like other details, it is an indicator of the type of management that exists. If a manager or supervisor permits his office, department, or shop to run haphazardly, one of the quickest places it will show up is in whether people come to work on time, are meticulous about coffee and luncheon breaks, and do not leave before the allotted hour. Scheduling of work is also indicated here as to whether deadlines are provided and there is insistence that they are met.

B. *Alertness to opportunity.*

(1) Obvious curiosity and inquisitiveness are to be found here.

(2) Specific suggestions as to how to do things differently and better and how to do different things.

(3) Evidence of specific improvements and accomplishment.

C. *Reliability.*

(1) This exists when you have perfect confidence that a manager's work is being well handled or he will let you know otherwise.

(2) When you feel absolutely positive that he will call upon you for help when he needs it and will give you help when you ask for it.

D. *Willingness to make sacrifices.*

(1) Here we find no complaints of overwork and no attempts to impress others with difficulty or length of work.

(2) There is evidence that he seeks and attracts additional responsibility.

(3) This person is not a clock-watcher.

(4) There is continuing evidence of adjustment of personal considerations, indicating a deep sense of responsibility and concern for the activities supervised.

E. *Appreciation of human values.*

(1) This is represented by a belief that people can be better than they are and can do better than they are doing.

(2) Evidence is found in specific training programs

which provide orientation, training on and for the job, and training for better jobs.

(3) Regular appraisals and discussion with subordinates about such appraisals give further proof of a belief in human values.

F. *Economic acuity.*

(1) Here we find belief in the dignity and validity of profit.

(2) This person operates at a profit when profit is called for.

(3) Economy is practiced in little things, as well as big ones.

(4) His financial demands are seldom questioned by superiors.

(5) We find no persistence here in demands for added expense when there is a lack of adequate funds, even though the added expense would be justifiable.

(6) Costs are reduced when specifically requested.

(7) There is constant impatience with loss items.

(8) This individual is not identified with extravagance.

3. A *philosophy and understanding of management.* This can be determined by simply asking for a written statement as to what a manager's basic thinking is on the following subjects:

- What management is, including a statement as to its responsibilities and obligations.
- What is his personal philosophy of life.
- What is his philosophy of management.

- What is his basic understanding of the economic philosophy of the system within which he works and of the political philosophy of the country within which he lives.

All this adds up to a clear-cut comprehension of the purpose and nature of business itself, of its place in modern society, and of the manager's place in it. This is within the framework of an understanding of the purpose of life.

4. *Management skills.* The possession of these can be ascertained by evidence of exercising them. Obviously, these are not all of the management skills, and any list that is set up for certification should be established to the satisfaction of those who engage in certifying.

A. *Long- and short-range planning.* This includes objectives and forecasting. All one has to do to certify the existence of this skill is to ask to see the long- and short-range objectives and the long- and short-range plans which the manager has. Ask for his forecasts, how he arrived at them, and what his record in forecasting has been. Does he operate on a budget, not only an annual calendar or fiscal year budget, but a moving budget that is always twelve months ahead? Does he, likewise, have broader five-year budgets toward which he is directing his thinking?

B. *Organizing.* This includes organization structure and the people in it. When trying to ascertain the existence of this skill, one asks for organization charts, position descriptions, activity analyses, job specifications, manning tables, and the like. He who possesses this skill knows all these things and can talk intelligently about them. He will have not only a chart of his present organization which is adapted to the personnel at hand, but he also will have his ideal chart toward which he is constantly working whenever a personnel change is possible.

C. *Appraising.* This includes standards of performance and specific measurements and controls as well as the ability to discuss the findings of such measurements with those appraised. The existence of this skill is ascertained by asking the individual what controls he has and uses. Without hesitancy he should be able to identify certain statistical, quality, production, financial, and personnel controls which enable him to know what is going on and to know it soon enough to take action when action is indicated.

D. *Decision making.* This skill is the ability to determine the correct decision, alternative decisions, and the timeliness of decisions. From the controls and measurements, certain things have been indicated about the course being followed as compared with the plans that have been set. The evidence of this skill is found in a lack of complaints by subordinates that they are not getting either decisions when they need them or the right to make them when they should have that authority which places decision making at the lowest possible level.

E. *Leadership.* This involves motivation and development. Here are found the powers of communication and inspiration. The finest indicator of the existence of this skill is the simple fact or evidence that his people are getting their work done as planned and desired. Another simple test is to change his job and to see what happens with the performance of the new group over which he has been given supervision. It will either go up or down; it cannot remain the same.

And so we could continue with many other indicators of mental condition, aptitudes, personal qualities, philosophies, and skills. It would seem, however, that enough has been said to make the major point obvious—specific items to be certified and specific means for certifying them are highly desirable. The next five years, particularly, will see a dramatic increase in specific, organized activity by management in the formal certification of managers.

One of the great problems today is that amateur and incompetent managers are pressured into using professional management techniques without skill or training. The result is fear, defensiveness, ridicule of the technique by managers, and disastrous impact upon the lives, attitudes, and work of employees.

The syllogism that because management is a profession, and because a man is a manager, he *is*, therefore, a professional manager is fallacious and dangerous. That is like saying that law is a profession; this man is a lawyer; therefore, he is a professional lawyer, even though he may never have passed his bar exam or been authorized to practice.

Managers of the future will have to meet certain tests and pass certain examinations. For this, they will receive a certificate properly authorized. This certificate will merely indicate that a person has met the requirements of the job. It cannot and never will indicate that he can do the job ably. It will simply say he has had preparation, without which he could not do it ably.

It is probably worthy of repetition that no one can develop a manager. No one can predict what he will do. We can, however, offer full opportunity for development and ascertain that he has what he needs to do the job well if he wishes to do so.

Let It So Happen

There are numerous ways of describing what a manager is, what he should know, and how he should operate. The continuing attempts to clarify management tend to establish that it is an activity in itself and that there is a great search for understanding of it.

It has been said that there are three kinds of people in the world—those who make things happen, those who watch things happen, and those who don't know what's happening. Managers are supposed to fall in the first of these categories because their specific function is to make things happen.

Managers do not wait for the future; they make it. As Henry Ford II has said, they do not react; they act. Managers can appraise themselves, therefore, or be appraised by others on the basis of what they have made happen that otherwise would not have occurred.

If something has to happen and a man is required to make it happen and it happens as it should happen, then the man on the job must be O.K. This is a manager's reassurance from a job well done.

It is necessary, therefore, that a manager know: (1) what has to happen; (2) what action is required to make it happen; (3) how it should happen; and (4) how it is happening. This may seem quite simple, but believe me, the statement is a loaded one.

For a manager to know what has to happen, he must have short- and long-range objectives. In helping others to understand what has to happen, he must put these plans in illustrated or written form. He also must use budgets, policies, and other management tools. He must be a master of communication.

If a manager is to know what action is required to make something happen, he must understand the elements involved in the assignment of responsibility: position descriptions, job specifications, activity analyses, organization charts, etc. He must be able to find, identify, obtain, and hold qualified people.

If a manager is to know how something should happen, he must provide expert guidance in the establishment of effective methods and procedures. He must be a master of the blueprint, of forecasting, of visualization, of experience analyses and technical know-how. Standards of performance, to him, are required for all jobs. He knows that every job must provide satisfactions from work relations and work output.

For a manager to know how something is happening, he must understand all types of controls, those that are appropriate for his use, appraisal systems, reports, and research. He must be conscious of measurement—its place, types available, and its value.

In addition to all this, a manager must keep people dissatisfied with the status quo and out of a groove. He constantly must instill in them the desire to do different things and to do things differently. A continuing sense of attainment must be the top reward for him and his people.

If a manager is a man of action who makes things happen and if, in order to do so, there are specific things he must know and do, then "let it so happen!"

What Do We Believe?

IF SOMEONE SUDDENLY FACED YOU WITH THE question, "What do you believe?" would you have any idea what your response would be? Would any fundamental beliefs immediately come to your mind in such clear form that you could respond without hesitancy?

The probability is that my first reaction, like that of most of you, would be, "Believe about what?" If the answer were, "About anything," would this help to bring forward more rapidly any basic belief?

The value of a belief is that it is part of the foundation of our lives. It is that upon which we can depend and which we are willing to stand by, regardless of the personal sacrifice that might be entailed. Character is a product of a foundation of faith which we have and which we are willing or not willing to defend.

It is appropriate that each of us identify, clarify, and periodically review what we believe (without any question of a doubt) about religion, government, the community, the home, the individual, and his work. Since these words will be read primarily by people in positions of responsibility in business and industry, let us first make an assumption and then conduct an examination.

Let us assume that, as managers in business and industry, we have clarified our convictions about religion, government, the community, the family, and the individual. The examination that follows has to do with determining what we believe in relation to our management responsibilities. Here are some questions that might help us in making an inventory of our beliefs.

Do we believe in the dignity and value of the human being?

Do we believe that with the proper assistance and motivation each individual is capable of more than he or she has yet disclosed?

Do we believe that institutions were created to serve people rather than that people were created for the sake of institutions?

Do we believe that the most effective management job can be done when individuals are given the greatest possible opportunity and assistance in self-development?

Do we believe in the validity and dignity of the profit motive?

Do we believe in the effectiveness and potential of the private enterprise system?

Do we believe in a fair day's work for a fair day's pay, and vice versa?

Do we believe that to have more we must deserve more?

Do we believe that, pretty generally, people are entitled to what they have, and that the way for all to have more is for more to be produced and created?

Do we believe that there can be no compromise with incompetency and no encouragement of mediocrity?

Do we believe that the public health and welfare rises above that of any individual or organization?

As I look at the questions written on my scratchpad, I think of several others that also might be mentioned. But the answers to the ones I have already submitted take care of the others, too. I might ask, for example, "Do we believe in the decentralization of authority and responsibility to the lowest level in the organization at which they can be handled intelligently?" Well, we have to believe that if we believe in the undeveloped potential of individuals. The convictions, therefore, about which I have raised questions are broad in scope even though specific.

Most religions have a prophet or prophets in whose lives can be found the answers to these questions. That is what makes religion a very practical thing and not just a matter of sentiment and emotion. We have to establish our basic convictions to be most effective in our daily work, and our religion can help us in determining what we should believe.

Just as important as believing something is representing that belief. Once we know what we believe, we know how to evaluate others who represent us in one way or another. We can question them on their beliefs, and if they are similar to ours, we should give them noticeable support.

In other words, all of us in positions of leadership should be willing to commit ourselves. What do we believe? What do others believe? How important is it that others whose beliefs coincide with ours receive our encouragement and backing? If what we believe is honorable, why should we hide it? If it is wrong, why should we not change it?

Let us, therefore, do at least three things: Select for ourselves those whose beliefs we wish to study as a help in determining our own; determine insofar as possible what we believe; support those who share our beliefs. The Christian message—unselfishness and selflessness—is a pretty good criterion for determining convictions worthy of support.

Only One Standard

THERE IS ONLY ONE KIND OF ACCEPTABLE performance—that which measures up to the highest standards. The highest standard for each individual is that which his conscience tells him is best. The best in terms of the individual's conscience is the result of his environment, associations, knowledge, and training.

Churches, schools, and other similar institutions are dedicated to the purpose of having an impact upon human lives that will continually raise individual standards. Most individuals then spend their lives striving to attain those standards.

In other words, continuing individual exposure to the impact of highly motivated institutions and people raises standards, and life becomes more and more of a challenge to attain higher and higher ideals. This is growth; this is life.

The attainment of standards requires motivation, courage, practice, and self-discipline. Inactivity, protection from exposure, constant avoidance of challenge will never get anybody anywhere toward the attainment of acceptable standards or contribute to individual growth.

While standards are always individual, there are many that are common to most personal codes. Most of them are not too difficult of attainment, and anything less is wholly unacceptable.

Most of us accept the desirability of being clean, neat, and proper about our personal being and appearance. This has nothing to do with economic status and is attainable by all.

Most sane people know that better health can result from specific effort to maintain it than from carelessness about one's physical well-being. This requires practice of habit-forming routines.

There seems to be little disagreement with the principle that it is good to be on time and to put in full time when time is an identified factor. Clock watching or "clock chiseling" is not in keeping with this ideal.

"A fair day's work for a fair day's pay" is a common slogan, and few would reject it as an acceptable standard. Meeting this standard takes effort and self-discipline but carries with it tremendous satisfaction. Any performance less than this is below standard and highly unacceptable.

Honesty, integrity, and reliability have never been proved to be anything but highly desirable. Since the beginning of time those who possess these qualities have been sought after.

A great majority of civilized human beings recognize the need for common courtesy and thoughtfulness in relation to others. It is generally accepted that graciousness is more desirable than boorishness.

Fulfilling one's responsibilities and living up to one's obligations are seldom denied to be admirable traits. Maintenance of such standards requires careful study of, and a continuing attempt to comprehend, responsibilities and obligations.

Identification with any thought or activity that sets people against people in a spirit other than that of true sportsmanship does not help anybody. Seldom is this ideal denied, but how frequently it is violated!

Goodwill is considered by most people to be desirable in human relationships. It is so important that the Supreme Court of the United States has defined it and it can be bought and sold.

Those who deny religion are simply trying to avoid a most common truth—that everyone is better for any attempt to live up to some religion. Religion never hurt anyone; running away from it is acceptance of a lower level of existence.

Many other standards could be named. We should give some thought to what our own standards are and how well we are living up to them. Humility involves a realization that one falls short of full attainment of the highest standards of life and a deep belief that anything less than attainment of these standards is unsatisfactory. No one, therefore, is perfect. To some this is a challenge, while to others it is an alibi.

How Do I Know I'm a Pro?

RECENTLY IT WAS MY PRIVILEGE TO PRESENT a concept of "The Present Status of Professional Management" to the entire management group of one company. During the discussion that followed, a foreman asked, "How do I know whether I am a professional manager?" The answer follows.

Get away by yourself, where you can do some prolonged and uninterrupted thinking. First, ask yourself this question: Am I on top of my job—am I in control—am I in command of myself and my work? The answer to this is to be found in the answers to other questions.

Are my work and that of my department guided by carefully worked out plans? Do I know what is to be done tomorrow, next week, next month? Have I any concept of or have I done any thinking as to the long-range future of the department? Have I outlined any specific measures to increase cleanliness and efficiency in the department, to reduce costs, to improve quality, to raise morale, to motivate my people to give of their best? *A pro knows what he wants to do and when.*

Do I know the company's policies affecting my department? Are there additional policies which I have created or should set up? Are these in writing and understood by those involved? A *pro clearly establishes the rules of the game.*

Is my department well organized? Does everybody know exactly what he is supposed to do, how much he has to do, and what his relationships are with other people? Do I have the best type of organization structure? This is important whether I have one person or fifteen working for me. A *pro is continually conscious of the importance of good organization.*

Do I have controls in the form of goals, standards, measurements, and built-in safety devices? A *pro knows that he has to have controls which will tell him what is happening, and some controls that will stop improper action automatically.*

Have I incentives and rewards which are properly related to work performance? Is my recognition of good performance timely, and is discipline for poor performance fair and firm? A *pro has the respect of his people because he recognizes their individual merit.*

Does my leadership inspire my people to give me the authority that I need to do my job? The greatest authority a manager can receive is that which comes from below. No one from above can equal it through edict or legislation. Is there anything specifically that I am doing which makes my people perform better for me than they would for someone else? A *pro is sensitive to the impact of his leadership on his environment.*

These are a few questions which will, at least, stimulate your thinking on the matter. It is doubtful whether your answer has been affirmative to all of them. If not, then the next answer to the question is that *a pro is a continuing student of management.* If you are providing and taking advantage of regular opportunities to develop yourself as a professional manager, then you are well on the way.

A pro has confidence in himself. This confidence arises from his vivid consciousness that his work divides itself into parts, each one of which requires know-how and skill. He fully accepts the fact that know-how comes from study, and skill comes from practice.

Visualize, if you will, a layman trying to perform a brain operation. Compare him with a knowledgeable, highly skilled, proven surgeon. The difference is obvious. The latter surely has more confidence in his ability to do the job at hand than does the former. Management is similar to and no less important than brain surgery. The impact upon human minds is through the use of other devices than surgical instruments. Just as much study, knowledge, practice, and skill, however, are required to have a motivating impact upon a human mind as are needed to repair some physical damage to it.

It has been said that someone once asked J. P. Morgan how much it cost him to operate his yacht. His answer was: "If you have to ask that question, don't operate one." Similarly, if a person has to ask whether he is a professional manager, he already has his answer. When he is a pro, he will know it.

Worth Every Cent He Nets

WHEN LARGE SALARIES, BONUSES, AND OTHER types of compensation for top executives are mentioned, one frequently hears a question asked: "How can a single individual be worth that much?" There is even sensitivity expressed by many executives about the reaction of stockholders to the compensation they receive. It is not at all uncommon for chief executive officers to refuse increases for themselves year after year because they do not like the direct or implied criticism that is identified with high income.

In the first place, I find that very few people who question large incomes have any comprehension of what taxes do to such incomes. Before we question a man's worth, in terms of dollar income, we must intelligently search out the facts about what he nets after taxes.

The average person in the United States of America, with a job income of $100,000 a year and a family of four, would net $55,276 after taxes. If he were to make $200,000 a year, he would net $84,776. If he received

$400,000 a year, his net would be $124,520. (When referring to "net," I am not talking in the usual terms of "take-home pay." Most people, when referring to their take-home pay, mean what they have in the pay envelope after the deduction of taxes, medical insurance, pensions, stock purchase, etc. When I refer to "net," I am referring to net after taxes only, because the other deductions are part of the income a man actually receives, even though he pays it out again for benefits.)

Someone immediately says: "Well, $124,520 is still a lot of money, and a man can't be worth that." But it should be remembered that he still does not get all of that in proportion to what people of lesser income get. A man at this income level undoubtedly has other income, and his net after taxes is, therefore, less. In addition, the financial demands upon him, because of his high income, are 'way out of proportion to the demands upon a person of lesser income. Gifts to relatives and friends, uncollectible "notes," charities, all chew into the income of a high-priced man. His own organization demands that he live on a higher level than he wants to in order to symbolize the success of the company.

Suppose, after all of this—after taxes, after charities, after gifts—a $400,000 man still nets $100,000; is he worth it? He's worth every cent of it, and in most cases chief executive officers are worth far more than anybody can pay them. They carry a type of responsibility and concern that cannot be bought in dollars and cents, and it frequently ends up in poor health and/or early death.

When one single person in an organization has the authority to make decisions that can break the company overnight, throw thousands of people out of work, even threaten the public welfare, this is something for which you cannot pay. This same person has the responsibility to make decisions that mean greater growth, more jobs, greater returns to investors, higher income for workers, and better goods and services to consumers. He does not pick these "off the top of his head." They are a result of skill, knowledge, intellect, deliberation, painful weighing of alternatives, continuous and deep concern. You cannot pay for this in dollars.

There is a very strange concept in the minds of many people to the effect that a company or an organization continues year in and year out, regardless of who heads it, or of his impact upon it. Practically every organized group of human beings is what it is, and where it is, and in the condition it is in, because of the capacity and the concern of chief executive officers, one at a time, down through the years.

When one tries to compare the dollar worth of the bricklayer, who lays down his job with his tools at the end of each day, with that of the president of the construction company, who has to maintain the opportunity for bricklayers to lay bricks each day, one is comparing apples with oranges. They just are not comparable.

When I hear that the chief executive officer of some organization receives a very high total income, my immediate reaction is not, "How can he be worth that much?" but rather, "He is worth every cent he nets."

Out of Context

ONE OF THE MOST UNFORTUNATE OF HUMAN practices is quoting or representing people out of context. This includes lifting a sentence from a paragraph, a paragraph from a chapter, or a chapter from a book or article. It could even include quoting someone without describing the circumstances or conditions within which a statement was made, if the circumstances have a direct bearing on the meaning of the statement.

Even if a quotation out of context is unintentional, it can, if the meaning is changed, be unfair, damaging, and even dishonest. The practice of quoting out of context is a common and disturbing contributor to poor communication between people.

If I should say, for example, "I do not like Mary," that has a very specific meaning. If, however, I say, "I do not like Mary in that dress," it has a completely different meaning. When I say, "I do not like Mary, least of all in that dress," three simple words give it still a different slant. It would be extremely important, therefore, that anyone quoting me repeat what I said exactly and entirely insofar as Mary is concerned.

If an executive says, "I do not like committees," that is a very clear statement that carries with it a perfectly understandable position on the part of the speaker. If, however, the same executive should say, "I do not like committee management," that has quite a different meaning. A third statement, "I do not like committees, least of all when they are used to run a business," has still a different implication.

If a listener has taken a position with regard to something, he frequently will listen for the kind of statement that supports his own stand. He is quite liable at times to take a little liberty in quoting another person by not repeating all that the person said about the subject.

Now that management has become a profession and, as such, places specific requirements upon those who are, or hope to be, members of it, there are many discussions and interpretations of it. There are perfectly natural attempts to rationalize one's own position in relation to it and to seek to qualify for the profession as one is, without any further effort.

Every question has its extreme positions, and individuals are prone to argue from extremes. Members of managerial groups range from the one-man dictator, who centralizes all authority in himself and asks no opinion of anyone, to the overly sensitized addict of group dynamics who waits for others to make the decisions. The former often is identified as typical of the non-professional manager; the latter embodies the concept commonly attributed to the professional manager.

Neither classification is correct, of course, and each is taken out of context.

A person says, "I am for the strong, dynamic leader." Well, who isn't? If, however, someone says, "I am for the strong, dynamic leader who makes all management decisions by himself," he would not find very much support.

A statement such as, "I have no use for the professional manager," would not get much of a following. If the statement were enlarged to say, "I have no use for the professional manager who abdicates his leadership to committees," very few would disagree.

It is just as misleading to generalize that strong, dynamic managers do not believe in or use consultation with others as it is to assume that a professional manager is a humanized nobody whose subordinates are meeting in continuous séances waiting for the spirit to move them.

The ultimate in management effectiveness is no different today than it has been all through history; what is needed now, and always has been needed, is the man who can get things done quickly, effectively, and to the complete attainment of predetermined objectives. This calls for a person who can set a course and then steer consistently in that direction, on schedule, regardless of conditions.

The difference is that the "do it yourself" manager does it the hard way. He struggles and strains and sweats while the organization waits comfortably and relaxed until he comes forth with the answers. The answers then have nothing to support them except the manager's confidence in himself, which, in most cases, can be pretty great. On the other hand, the professional manager obtains all the advice and counsel he can muster and then makes the decision. After all the consultation, he may still take action that only he believes to be right, but at least he has been exposed to several other courses of action and knows the reasons their proponents are in favor of them.

The professional manager gets things done in consultation with and through the efforts of other people. He realizes that others have much to contribute to his decisions, but he makes them and stands accountable for them. He also holds others, all down the line, responsible for decisions that have been delegated to them.

To imply that professional management is "softie" management and that the chief executive submerges himself in the identity of the group is to take professional management out of context. To imply that a strong leader is not a professional likewise takes the matter out of context. The best executive is a strong, dynamic individual, and the most effective strong, dynamic individual is a professional. It never will be otherwise.

PART THREE

The Organization and Its People

I have said that we find responsibility for management shot all through a business, that we find some degree of authority all along the line, that leadership can be exercised by many people besides the top executive. . . . The crux of business organization is how to join these varied responsibilities, these scattered authorities, these different kinds of leadership. For a business, to be a going concern, must be unified.

MARY PARKER FOLLETT
Freedom and Co-ordination

Staff and Line[*]

IT TAKES A GREAT DEAL OF INGENUITY TO ESTABLISH and maintain clear understanding and sound functioning of staff and line relationships. Few subjects in management generate so much heated discussion. Many of the human problems that arise in organizations can be traced to conflicts between staff and line.

The pendulum swings continually from one extreme to the other: too much power in the staff, which irritates the line and causes it to rebel; too much line independence of staff, thus causing the staff to rebel. It is extremely difficult to attain and hold a center position between these two extremes.

The most generally accepted concept of line and staff organization is not difficult to explain. It is less easy, however, to make it work because of human tendencies to absorb as much jurisdiction and power as possible.

* While this is written in an attempt to be helpful to those who work in staff and line organizations, it is not intended to imply that the writer believes this to be the best type of industrial or business structure.

The line organization includes those people who are engaged in the manufacture and distribution of the products or services for which the organization exists. The staff is engaged in those activities that assist the line in the attainment of its objectives.

The line cannot exist without the staff and the staff cannot exist without the line. They are equally important. While the staff and the line frequently deal with the same activities, their relationships to these activities are distinctly different.

The functions of the line organization are as follows: to set program and policy; to activate program and policy; to make the decisions and direct the organization required to attain the objectives of the organization.

The staff organization has the following functions: to help in the development of program and policy with the responsibility of seeing that they are adequate; to interpret policy; to make the finest possible tools available to the line for the activation of policy and program; to train the line in the use of such tools; to help in the selection and development of specialized personnel; to measure the effectiveness with which policy and program are applied; and to report results to top management.

This is "staff and line" in its simplest form. To say anything further complicates it, but one added point must be taken into account if serious lack of understanding is to be avoided.

While an entire organization can be set up on a line-and-staff basis, there can be line within staff and staff within line. The purpose of the company may be to manufacture and distribute washing machines. Those engaged in the manufacture and distribution are, therefore, line people. The purpose of the finance department is to maintain and protect the company funds. Within the finance department, therefore, which in itself is a staff department, there can be a line dealing directly with finances and supported by staff services within that department.

A commonly stated principle is that staff people cannot tell line people what to do. Theoretically that is so, but in practice it often is not. Staff people frequently can tell line people what to do because the line people have given the staff the responsibility and the authority to do so as a service.

The Internal Revenue Service can tell people when to pay taxes and penalize them for not paying because these same people have given the bureau that authority and responsibility as a service. It is a delegated authority from the line to the staff that can be rescinded at any time if enough people so desire.

Frequently a line organization will give authority to a certain staff department to administer a particular policy. The line agrees, for example, that uniform financial procedures must be followed throughout the organization if the company's funds are to be properly collected, protected, and disbursed. When the line has accepted the basic policies and procedures developed by the finance department, it then asks the finance department to enforce them.

If an organization is set up on a staff-and-line basis,

every supervisor, manager, and executive in it must clearly understand what that means and how it works. To the extent that such understanding is lacking, friction and strife will prevail. While this is only one of a number of phases of organization structure that should be understood by people in management, it is one of the most important. Great and immediate benefit will be derived from any time spent in training and discussion related to it.

Staff and line puts a premium upon management capacity because desire for power is accentuated by mediocrity and incompetence. That manager who cannot secure and maintain respect and confidence through his own personality and ability seeks some kind of authority to force people to accept his ideas.

The effectiveness of a staff executive is largely dependent upon his ability to influence others to accept his help and judgment. While many assume that a line executive has more inherent power and therefore commands greater obedience, this is not actually so. A line officer also is dependent upon others' understanding and acceptance of what he would like to have accomplished.

Leadership is effective only when it is desired and accepted by those who are subject to it. The greatest and most real authority comes from below.

The Other Fellow and I

In the many constructive discussions that are taking place these days on how to improve management effectiveness, one invariably hears comments such as the following: "How can top management be sold on attitudes and practices that are different from what they now follow?" "How can I get my boss to permit me to do these things?" "How can I get authority delegated to me commensurate with my responsibility?"

When top management or "the bosses" have such discussions, their questions are often just the opposite: "How can we get the various levels of management below us to accept, understand, and carry out our basic policies?" "How can we get our supervisors and middle-management people to accept responsibility and the obligations that go with it?" "How can we get people to do the things they should do?"

Here is a situation where individuals are concerned about getting their bosses to do what they think should be done, and where the bosses are concerned about how to get their subordinates to do what they should do. In other words, each looks to the other fellow as the stumbling block to his own greatest effectiveness.

While there is no question of a doubt that the other fellow has great influence upon our own performance, the opportunity still exists for us to do a lot for ourselves. A good question to face once in a while is, "What can I do that I should do despite whatever handicaps the other fellow places upon my performance?" Such an attitude sometimes results in the discovery that the other fellow and I are both after the same objective and are not in conflict at all.

A manager works in one of three kinds of situations: for a boss whose ideas and practices are in complete accord with his own; for a boss who is in partial disagreement with his ideas; or for a boss who is in complete disagreement with his ideas. An individual in management must operate in one of these three kinds of climate and he must guide himself accordingly.

If he and his boss are in general agreement in thought and practice, there is no problem, and the individual must concern himself only with producing to his greatest capacity. If they are in partial disagreement, the individual either must adapt himself to his situation or try to influence the boss. If they are in complete disagreement, and there is no possibility of either's viewpoint being changed, the individual must accept the boss's decisions or get out.

In any event, the first thing a person in management (and when I refer to management, I am talking about all individuals from first-line supervision to the top management level) must do is to consider how much he can accomplish by improvement in his own practices and procedures without coming into direct conflict with higher management. Those who feel that they do not have enough responsibility and authority should ask themselves if they are making the best of what they have. Sometimes, that is the best way to attain more.

If a manager cannot work with his people in certain ways because his actions are neutralized by conflicts with higher management practice, is he absolutely positive that he is getting all the results he should despite such a handicap? If an individual cannot do a management job under great difficulty, what assurance does he have of his competency when there are fewer obstacles?

Before we blame all our failures and frustrations on top management, let us be sure that we have made the most of our own abilities and that we actually have tested our bosses by attaining outstanding results by the methods in which we believe. Bosses, too, should ask themselves if they have done everything possible to get people under their supervision to accept certain standards and to perform in certain ways.

The inclination to blame our inability to accomplish certain things on the fact that the boss does not believe in them or on a subordinate's refusal to accept them actually diminishes our own effectiveness. If we shift our sights to doing everything we can as individuals, regardless of the difficulties, we sometimes discover that the difficulties disappear. Bosses are usually sold by successful performance, and subordinates usually measure up to responsibility and obligations placed squarely upon them.

Rather than looking for the weaknesses in the other fellow as an explanation of our difficulties, it might be wise to change our approach and first examine ourselves and our own performance.

Roaming the Ship

CROSSING THE OCEAN BY SHIP AND BY PLANE, I have been impressed by one particular practice of the officer in charge. When the sea or air is at its roughest, the captain is seen calmly roaming about the ship, chatting with the passengers, creating the impression that everything is well under control and that there is no reason for concern.

The captain can behave in this way because all operating activities on the ship are being handled by well-trained, competent people. That leaves him free to roam about as he wishes, when and where he wishes, to see that everything is in order. If the captain were at the wheel or the stick, he could not be anywhere else. Having a good pilot on the job, however, permits him to go from engine room to bridge at will.

Many executives seem to fear that the more they delegate, the less will be their contact with their people and their organization. There is an impression that by delegating a responsibility one removes himself from it completely. There is a concept that as a chief executive releases specific functions, he pushes himself up into the top of the triangle and becomes completely isolated there.

It is because of these unfortunate impressions that managers frequently ask, "How can I delegate and decentralize and still know what is going on?" The example of the ship captain is used in an effort to make it clear that delegation of responsibility actually frees the executive to have greater contact with his people and thus increase his knowledge of what is happening. The more functions he retains for his own performance, the more he is tied to his desk and to day-by-day responsibilities and the less opportunity he has to know his people and their activities.

An individual with a lot of functions to perform can give only part of his time to each of them. No matter how competent a person may be, he cannot give part-time attention to a lot of functions and do any one of them as well as even a less competent person could do that one on a full-time basis. The theory of decentralization, therefore, is that the executive gets rid of each of his functions as rapidly as he can to give himself greater freedom of action.

A useful measurement of our own effectiveness as executives is the extent to which we can relax in the realization that our work is being well handled by others. While the captain may take the wheel from time to time, he knows that when he does not, there is a competent pilot in that position. While he may occasionally step into the engine room and even operate some of the controls, he knows that when he is not there they are being operated and supervised as competently as when he is there. The captain may even walk into the radio room and start receiving or broadcasting if he wishes, but he isn't doing it because he has to. He's doing it only to get a feel of how things are working.

While freedom to roam the ship brings the chief officer closer to his people and has a beneficial effect upon their morale, at the same time he is very careful about what he does and what he says on such tours. Although he may and should listen to anyone who wishes to talk to him, he must be careful not to make decisions or suggestions that might undermine the position of the officers who are in command of the operations he is visiting. It is his right to roam and listen as he wishes, but it is not his right to interfere with the jurisdiction of the people to whom he has delegated responsibility.

In a plant or office, it is not difficult to sense whether the people are accustomed to the presence of the chief or whether they seldom see him. Those who are in the habit of seeing the boss are relaxed and casual about his visits. They know that he is around often enough to realize that they have their good moments and their bad moments and therefore will not judge them solely by what happens on a particular visit.

An organization that is not used to having the boss in its midst reacts with tenseness, caution, and frequently fear as everyone digs into his work with great vehemence. Sometimes mistakes are made under such conditions, and morale is lowered because of the impression made upon the boss.

There is certainly no dishonor in a manager's not being busy. The more casual, the more in evidence he is, the more effective he may be. In a well-managed business there is one final basis of judgment—the attainment of results. If objectives have been clearly determined in advance, if budgets have been set and approved after full participation by those who have to meet them, and if the goals set have been attained, then the manager has accomplished his job.

There are those who do the job with great stress and strain and those who do it with apparent ease. Do not be fooled by a casual or easy manner in an executive. He may appear to be just roaming the ship doing nothing, but if he is a good executive, his mind is active. He is observing; he is evaluating; he is planning corrective action; he is setting bigger and better goals. 'Way down deep inside he may even be worried and fretting, but he shows no sign of it. Such a person is really a great leader.

As rapidly as possible, therefore, let us build competent people to whom we can delegate as many of our specific functions as is right and reasonable. We then will be free to roam the ship, to know our people, to keep up with what is going on, and to get a real sense of how trim the ship is, how taut she is, how seaworthy for the voyage ahead.

Organization Sniffles

A DRIPPY SNIFFLE IS USUALLY A SYMPTOM OF a head cold. Common practice is to dry up the sniffle and live out the cold rather than go to bed, take proper medication, and cure the cold. If the sniffle continues for a long period, however, we begin to consider that it might be hay fever or something worse. We then test for allergies and go after the cause in a sincere way.

It would seem that symptoms of unhealthy organization structure have been in American business and industry long enough for us to take a careful look for allergies and causes. So many of the unpleasant symptoms have remained consistently with us that we should consider the possibility that the ailments are not temporary.

Some of the symptoms of unhealthy organization—some of the organization sniffles, so to speak—are: continuing and tenacious confusion in line and staff relationships and understanding; steadily increasing difficulty in controlling the number of managers who report to one executive without any intervening supervision—known as executive span of control; and the endless swing of the pendulum between centralization and decentralization. There are others, but these seem to be the most common and most frequently discussed.

It is possible and quite probable that we are allergic to military organization as it is applied to business. Since the military has done so much studying, research, and experimentation in this area, and since the only organization training that many business executives have had has been with the military, it is not surprising that military organization philosophy and practice have dominated business and industry. Compared with the military, the time, effort, and money expended by business in organization study are practically nil.

There is little doubt in my mind that the following statement will draw disagreement from many, but it happens to be a conviction, and I must, therefore, state it. Attaining military objectives does not require the same amount of individual judgment at all management levels as accomplishing the goals of private enterprise. When a decision is made at a certain military level, the main purpose of organization is to see that it is carried out with perfection, with precision, and on time. Little time is allowed for the exercise of judgment at lower echelons, except within a very limited range of alternatives.

Since there has been difficulty for so long in making line-and-staff organization structure work in business and industry, it may be right to conclude that it is not the best structure. Since decentralization is so hard to understand and to activate in private enterprise, maybe it has the wrong name and is conceived in the wrong way for civilian purposes.

Executive span of control, as we now understand it, forces us to think in terms of six, seven, or eight staff positions and one line position if there is an executive vice president and general manager; or possibly we think of eight or nine staff positions and the same number of line positions if there are operating divisions and subsidiaries. In any event, most top executives have more people looking to them for immediate direction than they should have, and there is continuing pressure for more.

When the chief executive looks at the organization structure, he frequently sees what he wants very clearly and understandably, but he shies from it because it is unorthodox and may be unacceptable to the technician. The organization structure, however, must be set up from the viewpoint of the chief executive because it is a medium through which he gets things done. Regardless of how unorthodox or what the form may be, the chief executive should feel comfortable in it and confident that it works effectively for him.

As I personally have the opportunity of studying this with more and more chief executives, I see a particular organization pattern becoming increasingly acceptable. On the other hand, I have not yet seen a chief executive who was daring enough to try it. Let us call it "executive organization" and see if we can describe it briefly.

A chief executive frequently thinks of his work as

divided into four segments: operations—the making and distribution of the product or service for which the organization exists; controls—the establishment and administration of policy and the setting up and institution of standard procedure required for desired uniformity; administrative services—that assistance which operations needs to get the job done; personal services—that which the president must do personally, or which has to do with him personally.

This would appear to be perfectly logical for organization charting. The chart would look something like this: At the top, under the board of directors, would be a box for the president. Below this would be three boxes for "Central Controls," "Operations," and "Central Services." Within the president's box would be found "Executive Services." Each of the three major divisions of activity—"Operations," "Central Controls," and "Central Services"—would be headed by an officer.

"Operations" would cover all functions having to do directly with attaining the company's objectives. "Central Controls" would be those activities such as plans, policies, measurements and inspection, budgets, accounting, standard procedures, engineering, insurance, wage and salary administration, and labor relations.

"Central Services" would include data processing, office management, employment offices, medical offices, training programs, and other services, including public relations, research and development, industrial and packaging engineering, etc.

"Executive Services" might be headed by a "Chief of Executive Services" or "Director of Executive Services" if the size of the operation justifies it. Here would be those functions that help the president in his own particular activities such as records and reports, analyses, special projects, callers, telephone, mail, transportation, and "office keeping."

Such a structure would enable the president to work with three major groups of activities and one group that is very immediate to him. This might mean only four or five people. These people, with the president, would be the coordinators—the integrators—those responsible for working out the relationships between people and departments that must be worked out if the organization is to operate successfully.

"Executive Organization," as described here, would cut out the power struggle between line and staff people; and this, in itself, would be a major contribution. "Operations" would be held solely responsible for doing the job for which the company is in business. It would have to get this job done within the framework of plans, policies, and standard procedures established and interpreted by "Central Controls," using the full help of "Central Services," which is centralized because it is more economical and more efficient that way.

Constant attempts to make the staff "purely advisory" and practically impotent would no longer be appropriate, and large amounts of time devoted to trying to "sell services" could be put to productive rendering of such services. Interference with the rest of the organization from members of the president's personal office staff would be inappropriate because of the clear understanding that they serve the president only and nobody else.

This concept I would neither argue for nor defend. I simply use it as an illustration of a clear organizational setup that does not rely upon many of the established principles of "staff and line" or "functional" structuring. Maybe there are other and more detailed ways of organizing, but at least I am convinced that we must tear ourselves away from military concepts and create some that are peculiar to and effective for business and industrial groups.

A Management Roadblock

ONE OF THE BIGGEST ROADBLOCKS TO HAVING the most competent management team possible is an inability, unwillingness, or lack of intestinal fortitude in handling problem cases. Some examples of problem cases are the following: fine, loyal, long-service employees who have rendered valuable service but can no longer meet the requirements of the positions they hold; individuals who have been promoted from positions in which they did well to positions which they cannot fill; individuals who are just plain incompetent; and individuals whose attitudes or habits make them undesirable.

Lack of action in regard to such problems often springs from a well-intentioned desire not to hurt people. While such a motive is most admirable, it does not always make for sound management. The failure to remove a person from a position, from which it has been deliberately and fairly determined he should be removed, might hurt more people than his actual removal. It is also possible that the removal of a person from a position for which he is not fitted might do him less harm than leaving him in it.

Practically every time one becomes engaged in a discussion of how to improve the effectiveness of a management team, questions such as these arise: What do you do with the competent, well-trained, young executive who cannot progress any further in the organization because of lack of opportunity? How do you protect the morale of an organization when old-timers who have outlived their usefulness are sidetracked? What happens when you have more good management material than you can use? What do you do with the "dead wood"?

Ways of meeting these problems are available to managers if they wish to use them. The problems are not at all insurmountable. There is sufficient proven experience to support the contention that these problems need not deter anyone in building the most competent management team possible.

First, the decision has to be made as to whether the incumbent of a management position is competent to do the job as it must be done. This requires a carefully worked out description of the responsibilities of the position and of standards of performance which reflect the results that should be attained by the individual in that position. Further, it requires the finest possible method of performance review which will permit arrival at a reasonably accurate and fair decision.

Secondly, if the decision has been made that the person in a job must be removed from it, the following question should be asked: Is there an individual in the organization who, in your judgment, can perform it as it should be performed? If so, the change should be made at once. If not, then immediate action should be taken to identify and prepare someone who can fill the position.

Thirdly, when the person is to be removed from the job, what consideration is he to receive? Should he be demoted to a position which he is able to handle? Should he be transferred to another position of equal classification which it is quite possible he could fill? Should he be terminated or placed on pension?

If the individual is to be terminated, is it for cause without consideration, or is there an adequate termination allowance which recognizes his years of service, his age, and his contributions to the organization? Should there be any effort made by the company to help him get placed elsewhere?

If he is to be placed on pension, is the pension adequate? Does the amount give proper recognition to the valuable services he has rendered, and is it sufficient to keep him out of immediate and serious economic difficulties?

There are two important phases to all of this consideration:

1. The rightness of the decision that a job can be filled more competently than it is being filled by the incumbent and that he cannot be developed to fill it.
2. The frankness, fairness, and sincerity with which the action is taken regarding what to do for the individual being removed from the job.

Having reached the first decision, the roadblock that stands in the way of taking action is usually that we have not provided the means of handling such a case fairly and adequately. We do not have carefully worked out and administered programs and policies of organization clarification, of appraisal, of development, and of termination allowances, pensions, provision for consulting services, etc.

When decisions about incompetency in management jobs are faced squarely, and when the means are available for fair and humane treatment of the individuals involved, then there are seldom problems of what to do with long-service people who have outlived their usefulness; with competent young people for whom there are no opportunities; and with the "dead wood" in an organization.

It would be most unfortunate if the implication were made here that the removal of such management roadblocks is a simple and easy matter. The responsibility for human lives is a tremendous one. Human problems have to be solved, however, for the sake of the health of the organization as a whole. And one of management's greatest responsibilities is to solve them.

No management should find itself in a situation where it has more good management potential than it can use for any extended period of time. If an organization has a person who is more competent to do a job than another, then that man should be put in the job. If there are competent individuals who can be of greater value than their present jobs permit and there is no job in the organization which they can perform more competently than the incumbent, then challenging jobs should be created through growth and expansion of the organization itself. This is the essence of company expansion and diversification. It is a wonderful position for a management to be in, but do not be too late in providing the opportunities and the challenge. If the team is too good for minor-league competition, then enter it in the big leagues.

Turning Over the Reins

"When will he ever turn over the reins?" "Why won't he turn over the reins?" These questions immediately convey an image. Reference obviously is being made to a boss who will not permit someone else to take over.

Statements of this nature bring to our minds a management situation in an organization. But perhaps there does not come to mind a clear picture of the original circumstances giving rise to the analogy of the driver's seat and the reins.

Visualize two men sitting on the front seat of a horse-drawn wagon. One man has the reins in his hands; he is the driver. Now, he passes the reins to his companion beside him. As he turns them over, he turns over with them the responsibility for driving the team.

When I visualize the driver of a team of horses turning over the reins to another, I do not see in this picture any action such as the following: the first driver retaining one rein; the first driver frequently grabbing the reins back; the first driver interfering with the reins while the second driver has them; the first driver giving instructions to the horses when he does not have the reins. Such actions do not come into focus in my memory because they did not occur in the heyday of horse-drawn vehicles, except in extreme emergency.

When one thinks of managers turning over the reins, however, the thoughts are blurred by such occurrences as these. It seems to be extremely difficult for a manager to turn over responsibility and let go. He may do it piecemeal; he may do it with frequent interference; and he may, from time to time, grab it back. He seldom does it in a clean-cut, confident fashion.

A growth company demands that managers turn over the reins. Frequently, this becomes necessary before the attainment of retirement age. There always comes a time in the growth of an organization when the genius, the methods, the creativity of the person who started the company and made it great are no longer possible. There comes a time when it is physically out of the question for the chief to know everybody on the payroll as he has known him from the beginning; to know everything that is going on in the organization as he has known it for decades; to spread his creativity to all points in the organization requiring creativity; to be available when necessary to make all the decisions that he has been making down through the years. It just cannot be done any longer!

How can the head of a business go about turning over the reins in an orderly and competent fashion? Having seen a particular pattern work successfully on numerous occasions, I would like to share it with others.

First, the chief executive must admit to himself that he can no longer run the business with the tight hand and the dynamic, creative leadership that he has had in the past. He just cannot spread himself that thin in view of the tremendous growth that has taken place under his leadership. He must now share it with others.

Next, he must identify the person to whom he will turn over the reins, and the sooner the better. There is much publicly announced objection to naming a "crown prince." There is no objection to crowning a prince, *if* the king has the courage to take the crown off when the prince does not make good. One of the advantages of crowning the prince early is that the king is still around to remove the crown if it does not fit.

How do you crown a prince in a business organization? First, you announce that *he* is in charge of the business when you are away from it. That means when you are away from the office; it does not mean that you still run it from your home, from some other office, from a vacation spot, or from some remote place on the earth. Somebody must be physically in charge at the headquarters of the company at all times, and when you are not there, the prince should be in charge. If you are both away, someone else should be so designated.

The next thing you do is to make the prince the chairman of your most important management committee. (This does not include an executive committee, which is a committee of the board and not a management committee.) Then announce to the committee that the prince has full authority to make decisions as a result of committee recommendations and/or discussion. Then work out with the prince those things that you would like to have discussed with you before he makes decisions.

List those matters that he must clear with you and upon which you are not willing to delegate full authority, and list them on paper. Some such items might be as follows: You will handle all official contacts with the board of directors; you will approve policies or changes in policies and submit to the board of directors those that have to be submitted; you will approve the budget for presentation to the board; you will retain final authority on all personnel changes for people making more than $12,000 a year; you will pass upon capital appropriations and budgets; etc.

Now is the time to turn over the reins and enjoy the ride. There isn't anything that says you cannot make suggestions, give advice and guidance. Make it clearly understood that there should be no hesitancy on the part of the prince to contact you at any time he wishes to discuss anything with you wherever you are, but do not make this imperative or a common practice for the prince to follow.

The pattern seems clear, but the determination must be doubly so. When the growth of a company no longer makes possible the personal methods of a chief executive who has made that company great, the time has come for him to consider turning over the reins, but this does not mean that he has to get off the wagon.

PART FOUR

Emphasis on the Individual

I swear nothing is good to me now that ignores individuals.

WALT WHITMAN
By Blue Ontario's Shore

You Cannot Miss

THAT MANAGER (FOREMAN, DEPARTMENT head, division chief, or officer) who consciously plans and works to give his people individual recognition cannot miss receiving a most rewarding response from them. In fact, this could be the major motivation technique a manager uses, because recognition and prestige are most important to individuals.

Nathan Hare, a young university teacher and former prize fighter, told W. C. Heinz in a *Saturday Evening Post* article of March 8, 1958 ("What Makes a Man a Fighter?") that while professional prize fighters "are all looking for financial reward, the greatest number are impelled even more by the desire for recognition and prestige. They long for the approval of the fans and for public understanding and acceptance." Don't we all?

Let us take a look at a few specific actions and activities that contribute to making individuals feel they are important. These are actual measures a manager can take without a great deal of effort, cost, or trouble.

About the simplest form of recognition of an individual is a nod when you see him—just some sign that you know he is there. If you add a smile, you've set him up for the rest of the day. Since few like to be ignored, consider the impact of being noticed!

If you can call a person by name, you're in. If you cannot remember or do not know his name, ask him what it is. He's proud of it. He's glad to tell you what it is even though perhaps you should have remembered it. He's delighted to be introduced by name to anyone who may be with you at the time.

Families are obviously important. If you know a man has a family, you know what to say. If you do not know, ask him. He's proud to tell about "the missus" and the kids. They're what he lives for or hopes for.

Next comes a man's job. Talking with him about his job, helping him with it, asking him about it, identifying its importance—all pay off. The real topper is when you can commend him for work well done. There are many special devices for this besides just a word from you to him: competition—individual and group; standards of performance against which he can measure his work; and incentive systems.

Then come the really tangible forms of individual recognition: increases in pay, promotions, service awards, suggestion systems, and titles. Titles are cheap, and they mean so much! It's amazing sometimes to hear fears expressed about passing out big titles that might spoil the recipients. It never hurt a good man to have his importance and prestige built up, and if he isn't good, don't give him *any* title.

Organizations! Have a lot of them. The more organizations, the more positions, the more offices to which people can be elected or appointed. The more offices, the more individuals who receive individual recognition. Even if they are not elected, those who are nominated receive a certain satisfaction out of that for a brief period.

You cannot have too many employee organizations with their own officers and directors to run the company recreation program, the cafeteria, special fund drives, the clubs to recognize many years of service, etc. This is an attractive feature of unionism; people receive recognition and prestige they otherwise would not get.

To satisfy human desire for recognition is not just an opportunity for a manager; it is a "must." People demand recognition. If they cannot get it one way, many will seek other ways. This is one reason it is most difficult to merge two or three struggling churches into one in a small community. In one church there are far fewer official positions for people to fill. This is also a major problem in merging companies. Instead of two boards of directors, there will be only one. One president replaces two. There may be only eight vice presidents instead of sixteen.

Whenever you reduce opportunities for individual recognition and prestige, you are in trouble. Whenever you increase such opportunities, you benefit. Does it not seem reasonable, therefore, that a manager should make every effort to provide recognition for his people? If he does, he cannot miss!

Before and After

DESPITE THE COMMON AND GENERALLY AD-mirable policy of "promotion from within," there are frequent occasions when it is necessary and/or desirable to hire people from outside an organization for key positions within it. One of the major reasons why such selections sometimes fail is the tendency toward overevaluation of the candidate just before employment and underevaluation just after employment.

The recruiting, interviewing, and employment process is a courtship. Before employment, or "joining," the candidate certainly is putting his best foot forward, and the company representatives usually are doing a selling job on him. Everything is sweetness and light.

The situation is analogous to the courting of Sis by a favored boy friend. He is on his best behavior, and the family may practice a way of life far above its normal habits. After the marriage, however, the members of the family unite in wondering how such a sweet girl could have married such a stumblebum.

The same thing happens when a college fraternity goes after a top member of the freshman class. The brothers really give him the works. They invite him to dinner. They all are dressed in their Sunday best, and the meal is one that would do credit to one of the world's most famous restaurants. Following dinner there is fine, elevated, broad, intellectual conversation. The house is neat and clean, and every room has its contents fairly well in place. After pledging, what a different life! What a shock the pledge receives, and what sheer joy the brothers get out of knocking him down to size. This seems to be human nature.

Similarly in a company, the first few weeks or months of work for a new employee seem to be a time for the "old" employees to jump on him to discover weaknesses that he has or even that he hasn't, to overemphasize and overdiscuss them, and to prove how inadequate he is. It is a strange phenomenon that people go so far out of their way to prove the correctness of their judgment when somebody is being selected and then try so hard to prove they were wrong after the selection has been made.

The way to handle this quite common problem in connection with the employment of outsiders is probably to discount the accepted evaluation of a candidate by about 30 per cent and then after his employment to discount the unfavorable reactions to him by about 50 per cent—at least during the first six months or year of his tenure. It is beyond ordinary comprehension to understand why a new employee at any level is expected to know, on the day he starts, everything known by other employees who have been with the organization for years. His most important lack of knowledge is in the field of relations with others. Instead of having to come to know and understand one new person, as do his new associates, he must come to know and understand many persons. He has to be almost superhuman in his human understanding.

There is one generalization in relation to all of this that, happily, you can pretty much rely upon. The good man ultimately comes out on top. A lot of wasted time and a lot of misunderstanding would be avoided, however, if we were a little more lenient in our judgment and gave him a little more encouragement. He might come out with fewer bruises and scars, and the rest of the organization might discover the quality of his contribution sooner than expected.

A Common Denominator

There is so much emphasis on the activity of management, because of the shortage of skilled managers and the increasing load on management, that we frequently overlook the highly essential services of the individual producer. In fact, a very common error by management is to make a poor manager out of a good individual producer.

Frequently, this mistake is caused by tenacious loyalty to a long-outmoded concept that no employee should make more than his boss. When one puts this situation into proper perspective, he realizes that were it not for the skill of individual producers there would be no bosses. I know of no professional sports manager who is not perfectly willing to have outstanding stars make more money than he does. I know of few business managers who are willing to have a top-notch engineer, scientist, or salesman make more money than they do.

Management is the only one of the major professions that requires a person to be a successful individual producer before he enters the profession. It is not only unwise but virtually impossible for a man to graduate from business school and immediately become a manager. He first must be a good engineer, a good scientist, a successful salesman, an acceptable accountant, etc. Doctors, lawyers, school teachers step right out of basic training into their professions because these are professions for individual producers.

A man is extremely fortunate when he has capable individual producers serving him. I consider myself among the most fortunate in having a highly skilled, competent young dentist. I have been spending many hours in his chair recently for a major "reconstruction" job, and I am fascinated by the way this man works. He tells me what he is doing and what he is going to do. He patiently explains it and illustrates it. I sit with a mirror in my hand and watch what he is doing.

This man hides no problems. He shrinks from no successes. He is quite outspoken about his disappointments and pleasures arising from the job. He is on the faculty of a neighboring dentistry school. He himself returns to school frequently for graduate work.

This dentist takes a great interest in me and my work, and we have talked much about the things I do—meetings from which I have just come, contacts I have just had the pleasure of making, etc. He knows that my business is management and frankly admits that he enjoys discussing certain aspects of it with me.

The other day, this dentist made the following observation: "It is rather interesting that when I was in college I participated in many leadership activities. I was president of my class, president of my fraternity, and held other responsible management positions. Despite this interest in leadership and apparent aptitude for management, I have become a dentist. This seems a bit puzzling."

Further discussion between us led to the conclusion that there is not anything peculiar about this at all. This dentist possesses a certain common denominator that would make him a success either as a manager or as an individual producer. In fact, it is a requisite of success to both. He is a teacher; he likes to teach. This gives him highly valuable communication, with anyone with whom he works, that inspires confidence and respect.

A good manager is a good teacher. A skillful manager who is also a good teacher finds himself classified with the best executives. This means he is extremely helpful to those who work for and with him. It cannot help but result in mutual understanding and respect.

A dentist or a doctor who is a good teacher, and who possesses the skill of his profession, is outstanding. He develops a communication with his patient that results in mutual understanding, confidence, and respect.

When one is a good teacher, therefore, he can be a good manager, and he can also be a good individual producer. The common denominator of which I speak is the ability to teach, to help to develop others. He who has this skill will undoubtedly be good at anything he tackles involving relationships with and responsibilities for other people.

Yesterday, Today, and Tomorrow

Today, as never before, there are continuing discussions and numerous studies aimed at determining the basic characteristics that distinguish a manager from others. Although there is no agreement as yet on any list of leadership qualities, there seems to be general concurrence on some individual characteristics.

One basic difference between the leader and the non-leader is that the former thinks of today's actions in terms of tomorrow's objectives while the non-leader takes each event as it comes, without concern for tomorrow. Since a manager is identified as one who makes things happen, he is an individual who instinctively thinks in terms of desirable objectives and who directs his activities toward their attainment. He thinks constantly of the future, and today's activities are handled more easily because the way to handle them was decided yesterday.

Unfortunately, far too many people have no concern for the future. They expect others to handle their emergencies for them as they arise. Also, far too many people are interested in getting as much as they can today without any regard for a mounting debt which their children will have to pay off. The effective manager has no such attitude.

It is not at all difficult to identify this basic difference in individuals. There is the person, for example, who carries very little insurance. If he is hit by a catastrophe, he seems to feel that his relatives, his banker, or some government agency should take care of the situation. He is the same person who does not budget his money or his time. When taxes come due, he hasn't the funds to pay them. When illness hits his family, he has no way to meet his obligations.

The manager-type person, on the other hand, plans his future needs and governs his time and income so that he can provide for those needs. This kind of person decides what he would like the future to provide and then works toward that end.

Personal experiences with two different financial executives come to mind. Their managerial competence was easily ascertained from the approach of each to the same activity—the daily determination of the company's cash position. The first executive paid the bills each day from the cash on hand. If the bills exceeded the cash, he either held the bills until they could be paid or he borrowed from the bank. He and his fellow executives frequently were subjected to emergencies because of sudden and sizable cash demands when there was a pitifully small amount of cash on hand. This man took each day as it came and did not plan his cash beyond today.

The second financial executive took a completely different approach. First, he was the most persistent member of the management team in his unremitting effort to perfect the budget from month to month and year to year. This was the basis of his determining future cash needs. When large amounts of money were needed at a particular time, he would distribute the amount over the days of the year prior to the date it was due.

For example, every two weeks this executive had a payroll to meet. Each day, he charged out of cash one-tenth of the payroll. Thus, when the day came to meet the payroll, he had the cash to cover it. He knew that every quarter he would be called upon to pay hundreds of thousands of dollars to the government for Social Security. Each day for three months in advance he set aside the proper amount, and that cash was available either in the bank or in short-term securities. This man seldom was caught by sudden surprises or emergencies.

This basic difference was brought home forcibly in a conversation I had with a young man who, in personality, physique, and intelligence, seemed to be endowed above the average. We were talking about profits and savings. It was suggested that it might be a good idea for any individual, regardless of the size of his income, to set aside some of it for future contingencies. The young man indicated that this was "that old-fashioned and outmoded concept of Yankee thrift."

When I asked who should take care of him if some day he were unable to do so himself, his immediate and unqualified answer was, "The government."

This conversation is cited to point out that, in my opinion, this man lacks an essential quality of management. I am not interested in finding out what other management qualities he might have because he has classified himself as a member of that group that feels no responsibility for the future.

One basic difference, therefore, between those who are of management caliber and those who are not is a sense of responsibility for the future and the capacity to plan that future and to meet current conditions in terms of their effect upon it. Such an individual can be identified as a planner, an organizer, a long-range thinker, who has responsibility and accountability.

In a situation, therefore, in which one is trying to evaluate the management potential or competency of another, find out why he is doing what he is today. If today's decisions and actions reflect yesterday's planning and are directly related to something he wants to see happen some months or years hence, then the man has at least one basic quality of a manager. If, however, he is not doing anything that is consciously directed toward the attainment of stated future objectives for himself, his family, his job, or his business, it would be a waste of time, in my opinion, to carry the evaluation any further.

"Pick Up My Marbles . . . . "

A COMMON EXPRESSION WHEN THINGS DO NOT go as one wishes is, "I'll pick up my marbles and go home." This has childish implications because it comes from childhood experiences. Adults are just grown-up children, however, and many characteristics stay with them through the years.

Back in the early days of my married life, my wife and I went on a lot of picnics with friends. I recall vividly an arrangement to go on a Saturday afternoon picnic with a young married couple who had a two-and-a-half-year-old daughter. The father was a rather well known child psychologist and college professor.

We assembled at the professor's home, as scheduled, to leave on the picnic. The whole group was held up for two hours while the parents of the two-and-a-half-year-old child tried to get her to "want to go on the picnic." For some reason the child did not "want to go," and the philosophy in that household was that no one should do anything he or she did not *want* to do. It was supposed to repress one's personality in some way that would crop out disastrously in later years if a child were forced against its will to undertake a distasteful task or perform an onerous duty.

This philosophy has spread throughout many management circles during the past decade. There are all kinds of techniques being taught today that supposedly help a manager get people to want to do what the manager wants them to do. It is broadly believed that if you have an idea you want others to adopt, the best way to get them to adopt it is to wait long enough for them to arrive at the idea themselves.

Some people call this management by consent. The basic theme of it is that we should get people to do what they should do because they want to do it. This is a sound philosophy, but what should be done by a manager when one or more of his people do not want to do what must be done? One of the finest aspects of life is that we are called upon to do things that we do not necessarily want or like to do. This is what contributes to character, to maturity, to self-discipline.

Most managers do not want to refuse pay increases, but there are times when they must; they do not like to refuse extra employees on the payroll when requested by subordinates, but there are times when they have no choice. The same people do not like to turn down requests for more office space, more or better furniture, bigger cars, etc. There are times, however, when they have to do these things even though they do not want or do not like to do them.

Profit margins in business and industry must be maintained or increased. In order to do this, there are a lot of new expenditures that have to be denied. Business conditions are such that time is not always available to persuade people to accept the proposals they do not want to accept. Fact is fact and, when this is not accepted, there are some limitations to be placed upon disappointment and patience.

The philosophy that no manager should do anything he does not want or like to do, or should not ask others to do anything they do not want or like to do (to the exclusion of any other approach), is one of the contributors to the growing concept that management today is getting a bit soft. Surely, when anybody adopts this as a single philosophy, he *is* getting soft. When something has to be done, the manager had better get it done. And if time does not permit persuading a two-and-a-half-year-old child that she wants to go on a picnic, someone should pick her up in his arms and take her.

That adult who is permitted to delay appropriate action with self-styled importance, fed by the belief he must be "sold," should be limited in the time made available for this purpose. Furthermore, he should not be given the opportunity to "pick up his marbles and go home" unless it is clearly understood that he is not expected back. He can keep his marbles and stay at home!

There's Quite a Difference

THERE IS QUITE A DIFFERENCE BETWEEN A person who simply deplores a condition and a person who is responsible for eliminating it. It is strange that so frequently the person who has the responsibility for eliminating the condition is blamed for its existence.

People are universally against cancer. The medical profession has the responsibility to eliminate it. It is odd, therefore, to hear members of the medical profession criticized as if they had created the disease they are fighting. People are pretty generally against illiteracy, and educators are responsible for eliminating it. Yet, many times, educators are highly criticized for the very illiteracy they are combating.

Practically everyone is against high taxes—at least everyone who has to pay them. Those who have no responsibility for the government operations that require taxes for support are in a completely different situation from those who are responsible for the collection and expenditure of tax moneys.

In other words, it is easy to criticize, to deplore, to be against what is undesirable, but it is quite different to be in a position of responsibility for eliminating it. The fact that a person is busy in the elimination of undesirable conditions and does not spend his time speaking out against them does not mean that he deplores them any less than the person who is free to do nothing else but.

What is the point? The point is this: One frequently hears individuals preaching vehemently against unemployment and blaming employers for it. If those same individuals were employers responsible for providing hundreds and thousands of jobs and for keeping people employed, they would find themselves in a rather different position. They would be no less critical about unemployment, but they would talk less about it because they would be constructively occupied in creating and maintaining employment.

Visualize, if you will, an employer of 3,000 people. He maintains the jobs for those people. His capacity to meet the payroll depends upon the income of the business. If the income is not sufficient to meet the payroll for 3,000 people, he has at least two choices: He can continue to meet the payroll until he has used up his credit, gone broke, and 3,000 people are out of work; or he can reduce his payroll by releasing one, two, or three hundred people, and thereby save the business, maintain the jobs that remain, and retain the possibility of once again having jobs for those who were laid off.

It is disturbing, to say the least, to hear criticism of those who create, protect, and pay for the employment that exists. The implication by these critics is that employers are pleased by unemployment.

Every employer would like to be able to hire more people, to pay for more jobs. This would mean that he had a bigger and better business. I never knew an employer who was happy about reducing a payroll, a teacher who was happy about illiteracy, a doctor who was pleased about cancer, or a government official who was glad about high taxes. These people, however, do not have the time to speak out against the conditions they deplore; they are devoting their lives to trying to eliminate these conditions.

There is a basic difference between lack of responsibility and responsibility. The person who has no responsibility is free to shout about what is wrong; the person who has the responsibility must be occupied in doing something about the problem. Let us be most careful not to accuse those who are working for the elimination of undesirable conditions of being the ones who created or who condone these conditions.

Don't You Believe It

Most of us realize that good health and long life are greatly enhanced by regular daily exercise. Beyond middle age, however, few of us exercise regularly. We also know that good eating—regular eating, proper diet—enhances our health, keeps us at proper weight levels, and reduces our susceptibility to disease. Most of us, however, are quite reckless in our eating habits.

We know that in order to think well, in order to weigh facts and arrive at sound decisions, and to be able to think quickly and ably, we must think regularly. Just as good exercise and good eating are essential to good health, so regular thinking is helpful to our overall intellectual capacities. In other words, our minds have to be exercised just as our bodies do.

Despite this clear knowledge that we possess, most of us do not exercise our minds very regularly or frequently. We are mentally lazy. As a result, we are inclined to accept certain common statements as truth without weighing or examining them. It is amazing how much we accept as true that is actually not true.

As a result of this mental laziness on the part of many people, we play right into the hands of individuals who are intently dedicating themselves to the dissemination of ideas quite contrary to those we believe. We frequently put ourselves on the side of our ideological enemies by accepting something as truth that they want us to accept as truth, thereby placing ourselves at a disadvantage.

Those who appeal to the selfishness of individuals—those who want to further the welfare state, those who wish to expand the philosophy that individuals should receive according to their need rather than their merit—are very pleased with the realization that a certain statement is commonly accepted by those who should believe otherwise. This statement is to the effect that human beings would prefer to receive something for nothing rather than work for it. By getting people to believe this, those who promise something for nothing have the most popular appeal and will, therefore, get the greatest following. But I *don't* believe it!

As I know people in all walks of life, I am quite convinced that, basically, people do not want to receive something for nothing. People really would like to be of some value. They want an opportunity to do something, to earn something, to possess something that they deserve because of their contributions.

If the average man is given a choice between an opportunity to be of real value and to attain something significant, as against receiving something for doing absolutely nothing, I feel quite positive that he will accept the former alternative. The problem has been that people are not given sufficient opportunity to render service of value and, therefore, in frustration, fall victim to the offers of people to receive something without contributing.

It is my humble belief that management, which is commonly supposed to stand for the philosophy that people should produce and share according to their productiveness, has been responsible for many people's accepting welfare rather than working for what they receive. Many managers, over the years, have been too prone to treat employees as groups—to level off productivity and opportunity, and to ignore individual potential.

The basic skill of a manager—more important than any other skill—is inspiring, motivating, helping, and building individual workers to produce high quality, high volume at low cost, because they *want* to. Because managers have not exercised this skill adequately, too many employees have not had the opportunity to be of real value, to do their best, and to contribute to significant accomplishment.

What this boils down to is that the average person is offered two schools of thought, two directions to take in his basic philosophy of life: working to contribute, and sharing according to his contribution; or receiving according to need and, therefore, contributing nothing so the need can be greater. The only people who can offer him the first choice are his bosses. If they do not offer him this first choice, then he has only the second. He has to turn to those who offer something for nothing if he is not given the opportunity to do something of real value, or at least to try to attain his fullest potential.

When it is said, therefore, that people would rather receive something for nothing than work for it, don't you believe it. I think many people are willing to accept something for nothing only because they are not given sufficient opportunity to produce to their greatest potential.

Courtesy and Customs

THERE ARE MANY INSTANCES IN HUMAN RElationships when perfectly competent people fail in their assignments because they have unnecessarily offended someone. We constantly hear of such offenses being caused by language barriers and variations in background, culture, and customs. A basic approach to avoiding this kind of mischance is to develop a keen sensitivity toward other people and their feelings.

On many occasions a skilled government representative visiting some country, with a relatively easy mission to perform, has been known to bungle the whole affair because of failure to observe a local custom of some import to the natives. In fact, such an incident has sometimes strained diplomatic relations so much that it has taken years to straighten them out.

Business men with proven ability to do a certain type of work have often failed miserably when called upon to do it in other lands, simply because they have openly violated some local code of conduct. This has occurred not only when a person was shifted from one country to another but also when he was shifted from one community to another within the same country.

To bring this whole matter down to a much closer focus, consider the friendships that have ended on the rocks simply because individuals did not observe the customs and practices prevailing within each other's homes. People are inclined to be adjusted to and to like the habits, practices, and environment within which they have been brought up and to which they have become accustomed. When a visitor, innocently or deliberately, does something that openly clashes with the environment in which he finds himself, this rubs people the wrong way. At the same time, it seems so unnecessary.

If one is visiting a country where the custom is not to smoke at a meal until the sovereign has been toasted, one who violates this custom is not looked upon with favor. When one is in a community where the custom is for a man to offer a lady a seat on a public conveyance, he who does not do so is an object of notice. Even though a person has been brought up in a home where the habit was to gulp one's food and get away from the table as fast as possible, it is good to relax and remain for a considerably longer time at the table in the home of those whose practice it is to eat more leisurely and as a family.

A sound ruling, of course, is provided by the age-old saying, "When in Rome, do as the Romans do." If, however, when you get to Rome you do not know what the Romans do, then how can you be reasonably sure you will not offend someone? A basic approach is this: Be sensitive enough to observe what other people do;

be curious enough to listen and watch before speaking or acting. Considerateness and courtesy never got anyone into serious trouble.

When this problem is discussed, particularly in relation to the failures of business men and government representatives in other lands, it is often suggested that courses of instruction and orientation would be very helpful. If people could be trained in the culture and mores of other people before they visited them, they would be less likely to violate the sensibilities of their hosts. This idea is indeed worthwhile, but frequently time, circumstances, and economics make it impossible.

Desirable as orientation and training are, much as they will help, there is a great deal that can be done without them. Just be sensitive enough to other people to notice what they say and do before doing or saying things that conceivably might be offensive to them. This, of course, is difficult for a person who is not normally sensitive to the thoughts and feelings of others. For a person who is habitually discourteous to others and inconsiderate of human feelings, this basic approach requires considerable self-discipline.

Those who are not sensitive to others probably will make bad mistakes regardless of where they are or what orientation they receive. Perhaps, therefore, all of us, in all situations, should try a little more consciously and a little more continuously to develop basic habits that make us more observant and considerate of the other fellow.

As Others Think You Are

ONE OF THE MOST COMMON PHRASES HEARD today is: "It's what you are that counts." This always strikes me as a bit puzzling, and its rightness depends upon one's interpretation of "what counts."

No one knows what a person really is like as well as he does himself. This secret knowledge of what he really is counts only to himself. Whatever help or satisfaction this gives him, or whatever regrets, remorse, or complexes it develops within him, is quite a personal matter.

There could be some question as to whether what counts to a man is as important as what counts to all men and women with whom he has contact. What really counts to other people is what they *think* a man is rather than what he really is. They may frequently think him to be better than he is—and that's good, not bad!

Many doubts are expressed about the value of personnel appraisal work because of its questionable accuracy. If one person, in an appraisal of another, says the second person does not have good judgment, someone is immediately inclined to ask, "How do you know he doesn't have good judgment?" or, "Are you right that he doesn't have good judgment?"

Whether the individual appraised has good judgment is not so important as the fact that he who appraised him does not think he has good judgment. His judgment, therefore, has little value in relationships between him and the appraiser just as long as the appraiser doubts the value of the judgment of the appraised.

Some executive makes the statement that one of his key managers is not technically well informed for the position that he wants. Whether or not he is technically well informed is not what counts. What counts is that his boss does not think he is. Appraisals indicate what people think about other people, and the fact that they think it does not necessarily make it true. Neither does inability to ascertain the truth make the appraisal of another's thoughts any less valuable. The basic purpose of an appraisal is to ascertain what certain people think about certain other people. This is the base from which to improve human relationships and human performance.

In cases of this kind, what an executive does is more important than what he is. What other people think he is is more important than what he actually is. In its simplest form, this means to you and me that it is the practices a manager follows that really count. As someone once said: "What you do speaks so loudly I cannot hear what you say."

A particular situation in my own experience found a number-two executive in a company bypassed three times in six years for the job for which he was logically in line. He could not understand this and pressed his superiors into making an appraisal of him. The result of the appraisal disclosed that his superiors had not selected him for promotion "because they did not have confidence in him." The victim in this case argued at great length to the effect that lack of confidence in him was not justified. It took considerable patience and effort to convince him that this was not what was important. What was important was that those whose judgment of him counted did not have confidence in him. *That* was the fact. With this he could not argue.

It is just as important that an individual be continually conscious of the image that he is creating in the minds of other people as it is important that a company be concerned about the image its public has of it. What we really are is of importance to us. What others think we are, and expect us to be and do, is important to the world about us.

Keep the Pressure Down

WRITING WORDS OF ADVICE AND MAKING VARIous observations for publication have as a by-product some soul-searching by the writer. When deliberating upon certain themes, self-application is unavoidable.

Time and time again, a particular problem of managers comes to my attention. Time and again, I have wanted to write about it. Because I am guilty of that which I am about to point out, I have feared that I might believe it to be more prevalent than it actually is. There has been too much evidence, however, of similar practices on the part of others for me to hide my own guilt longer.

Many managers permit irritations, created by their own people, to go too long before discussing them with those involved. The manager will build up a terrific head of steam, carry the burden for weeks and months, before he will discuss his irritation with the person who causes it. Frequently, he never does. He hopes for some development to cause the removal of the irritating person before he has to face that person with the irritations.

The average manager does not like to bawl people out. Neither does he have the skill to arrive at helpful understanding without appearing to scold the person. Furthermore, too many people consider any suggestion from a boss as a bawling out.

It is extremely difficult to discuss unsatisfactory performance with someone without having that person feel that the whole world is falling apart and that the boss is completely dissatisfied with him and everything he represents. Frequently, what is irritating the boss is a very minor part of the individual's work, but if permitted to go on indefinitely, it becomes a major problem.

Consider the worker who is chronically late; every morning, he comes in five, ten, or fifteen minutes after the bell has rung. He just cannot keep his rest period or coffee break within bounds. It is usually this person who is ready to leave and standing at the elevator when the closing whistle blows.

The boss knows this; he sees it; and he doesn't like it. He feels the individual worker ought to know it is wrong and that he, therefore, must be doing this intentionally. He feels awkward about saying anything to the worker about it because it probably will not be received well; it might affect morale; and he might even tell the boss what he can do about it. Day after day passes until everything this worker does is colored by this irritation on the part of his manager.

Another worker just will not be clean and orderly about his work. It seems to make no difference how many different ways you approach him. He just cannot be neat—or just will not be. On the other hand, neatness is a vital part of the job. The manager tries all kinds of schemes to get the worker to mend his ways without criticizing him head-on, but the worker does not tumble.

To the hard-boiled manager, this all probably seems quite ridiculous. There are managers who, because of their incompetency, rule by force and care not who thinks what about what they say or how they say it—"If the workers don't like it, they can lump it." The skilled manager, however, is very sensitive to the reactions of his people. He wants to get the best out of them and does not want them to misinterpret or improperly evaluate his reactions to their work.

Maybe the answer to all this is that he should not carry burdens of irritation. When a person working for us does something that is irritating, maybe we should discuss it right at that point before the practice grows into a habit and before the irritation grows into an ulcer.

We want understanding with our people; we want to be helpful to them in their development as producers. Whatever we say, regardless of how trivial, should be discussed immediately for purposes of understanding. Even if we hear anything that causes irritation on our part, we should investigate it immediately.

If this is our continuing practice, or continuing philosophy, or continuing approach to our people, maybe it is possible that they will not misinterpret our criticism or, better yet, our suggestions. I pray for the day when I can do this better than I have yet been able to do it. I am inclined to suffer too long over what I consider to be the wrongdoings of other people.

Maybe, if I face the issue immediately when it arises, I will find out that it is not anywhere near as serious as it looks and that possibly I am the cause of it. Maybe I have not made clear the standard of performance I expect, and maybe I am expecting old habits, developed under other managers, to be dropped overnight under my leadership. At least, I am going to try to keep the pressure down by letting off the steam more frequently and sooner.

Seasoned Troops

MUCH ATTENTION IS FOCUSED UPON THE PERson whose current performance is exceptional. In our continuing, almost frantic search for management talent, we tend to emphasize dynamic, creative producers. This is all right if it does not keep us from appreciating the value of long experience within one organization.

Any organization requires individuals of unusual and scintillating capability, but at the same time one of its greatest assets is its seasoned performers. Those individuals who have been around for many, many years represent a vast amount of know-how that is irreplaceable.

When you read or hear about seasoned troops going into battle, somehow you have a kind of confidence that you otherwise lack. Here are men who have had long, hard experience. They have been in the front lines many times. They know what to expect and what to do about it. There is seldom confusion and never is there panic among seasoned troops.

Certain procedures, routines, disciplines, and traditions exist and function within an old organization without written directions or constant supervision and checking. This is because of the old-timers who grew up with them, understand and accept them, and pass them along to the newcomers without obvious effort or fuss. The newcomers have respect for the "old pros" and accept their help and suggestions as a matter of course. Many things that move along smoothly without question when seasoned troops are present create a furor when all troops are green, for each man thinks he knows as much as the other and everything is subject to dispute.

This is one of the basic problems of new or rapidly growing organizations. There appear to be much confusion, constant issuing of new instructions and procedures, and some feeling of unsettled morale at times. This is because routines and disciplines that have long since become established practice in old organizations have yet to be instituted in the new ones.

As a rather oversimplified illustration of the point I am trying to make, consider the company switchboard with four operators who have been in the company five to fifteen years as compared to the switchboard with four operators who have less than six months' service each. Think of the confusion, the errors, the lower quality of telephone service in the latter case as against the former.

Visualize what happens to a newly hired operator in these two situations. It is obvious in which she will learn the most with the greatest speed and with the least fuss and feathers.

Emphasis on the Individual

It would be literally impossible to put into standard procedures, to incorporate in an operating manual, or to include in a training course all the knowledge of company policies, of procedures and practices, and of executive personalities and peculiarities that the long-service operators have accumulated over the years. These girls know more about what is going on than anybody else; compared with them, the newer operators are at a distinct disadvantage. (This is not intended as a reflection upon the newer operator, but rather as a tribute to the one with greater experience.)

Think, too, of the accumulated experience in human relations. Few have to put up with so many unpleasant human characteristics as do telephone operators. In few jobs are there so many temptations every day to speak one's mind. Only experience teaches the girl at the switchboard to remain calm and courteous under fire.

Many times we overlook the inherent golden value of experienced people, whatever their rank or status in the organization. The more of them we have, the less supervisory time is required for basic training and the more training takes place by mere association with them. Look with reverence at the old-timer, the old pro, the long-service employee. He is a steadying influence; he is the backbone of morale; every day, quietly and almost unnoticeably, he is performing a function that is horribly missing when he is not around. There is absolutely no substitute for seasoned troops.

Believe It or Not

FEW PEOPLE IN THIS WORLD ARE BY NATURE cruel, ruthless, and hard-boiled. Those who appear that way are usually compensating for something. Most often they have to do something they do not want or like to do and are doing it in what seems to be the easiest way.

There are times when managers have to dismiss people from the payroll. Sympathy immediately goes out to the dismissed, and the impression commonly becomes prevalent that the manager who took the action was thoughtless, tough, ruthless, and cruel.

Believe it or not, the average manager today is deeply hurt when one of his employees fails to measure up. He worries and frets about it. Usually it is on his heart and mind for weeks or even months before he takes the action that his responsibility requires him to take. It is anything but an easy and pleasant experience to tell some individual that he is no longer needed or wanted and that his income ceases as of a certain date. It is difficult regardless of how wrong the person dismissed may be.

In my own rather close association with managers for more than a quarter of a century I have seen more people who should be dismissed remain on the job because of the manager's unwillingness to face up to the situation than I have seen individuals unfairly dismissed. I know of no decision that receives as much consideration, study, and concern on the part of most managers as does the apparent necessity for dismissing somebody.

The act of dismissal is a peculiar responsibility of a manager. A non-supervisory person, who never has to do this, cannot possibly understand the effect it would have on him. Many managers cannot take this action because they cannot face up to it—it hurts too much. But often it hurts worse to continue someone on the payroll who should be dismissed.

Think of the sequence of human relationships and emotions in the following incident. A foreman has a position to fill. With the help of the personnel department he picks out the best of the available candidates. He likes the man. He introduces him around the job and helps him get started. He goes out of his way to try to assist the new employee; the employee responds well and attains performance standards rapidly and skillfully.

The foreman is proud of this new employee and of his performance and is glad to have him on the team. The foreman's emotional reaction is much the same as that of a football coach who sees a rookie do well in his first game.

Then, gradually, something begins to go wrong. Perhaps the employee becomes overconfident, or he develops some other unfortunate attitude, or the machine he is operating is replaced by one requiring greater skill, or the standards are raised beyond his competency—something happens that makes him a problem case. The foreman works hard to solve the problem, consults with the general foreman, does everything he can, but nothing works; this employee has just gone sour. It is finally determined that he either cannot or will not perform satisfactorily. At that point management, having tried everything else, has only one alternative, dismissal.

Here is a tremendous change in emotional reaction to another human being. This is a man of whom the boss was proud but who has become a great problem to him and now has to be fired. Anyone who thinks that the hours and days preceding the dismissal are easy ones for the foreman is indeed mistaken. The chances are the strain on him will be reflected in his relationships with his family, with his associates, even in his job attitude and performance. Perhaps, being unskilled in handling things of this kind easily, he may get tough about the dismissal. In his efforts to protect himself against probably unfavorable reactions from other employees he may appear a little cruel.

Exactly this kind of situation can develop at the top of an organization between officers and department heads. It may be even more difficult because the relationships are often longer and closer. The families probably know each other and may have been on social terms. Perhaps their children have gone to school together. Ultimately the time comes when some person fails to measure up. Everything possible is done in discussing the problem with the individual, in considering what help might be given to improve his performance, in considering other job responsibilities that he might perform more satisfactorily.

If all these efforts fail, the day comes when the decision is obvious—the relationship with the company must be severed. He who does it faces immediate criticism from those who do not know the facts. Nor is it decent or good sportsmanship for the one who does the dismissing to spread the facts. Regardless of what the one dismissed may say, it is not considered good management for an executive to publicize the inadequacies of his subordinates. He therefore fulfills the responsibility, absorbs the criticism, and perhaps seems a bit hard-boiled about it because he cannot and will not discuss it.

The manager's job is not always so desirable as it appears. It carries great responsibility. It requires him to take certain actions that he is not always in a position to defend. It sometimes requires, for the sake of the organization and the people in it, that some individual be hurt. There is a common saying attributed to the father who is spanking the child, "This hurts me worse than it does you." Believe it or not, in most cases that is true.

PART FIVE

Jobs and Job Performance

He who does something at the head of one regiment will eclipse him who does nothing at the head of a hundred.

Abraham Lincoln
Letter to General Hunter

Performance Standards for All

Although the introduction of work standards for production workers was originally resisted by both management and labor, these groups now generally accept the principle of standards of performance. Management and labor together have learned how to develop such standards intelligently, how to introduce them, how to obtain workers' understanding and acceptance of them, and how to apply them.

There is, of course, continuing resistance to the raising of standards as performance improves, but this is perfectly natural. Were there not such resistance, there would be those who would raise them too fast and too high, and this could lead to the exploitation of a very fine principle and technique.

Work standards are very specific; they are engineered. Performance is definitely measurable against the standards, and evaluation is a matter of mathematics. When we have established what a unit of work is and how many units have been produced, we have a set of facts about which there is no question.

During the past few years, interest in the development of performance standards for all people in an organization, as well as for production workers, has been growing rapidly. A great deal of activity is going on in an attempt to develop standards for everyone—supervisory, management, and administrative personnel; specialists; scientists; copywriters; etc. We are, of course, experiencing the same resistance, the same confusion, the same doubts that were in existence in the early days when production line standards were being worked out.

There is the same desire to be specific, to find standards that eliminate human judgment about performance, and to make twelve inches equal one foot without the variance of a hair. Many people feel that a standard is not a standard unless it is a specific measurement with which performance can actually be compared, and this position is perfectly reasonable. It is my impression, however, that this insistence upon exactness in the determination of results may be delaying the use of a very effective tool.

The example usually raised by those who question the advisability of performance standards for all is that of a research worker, a scientist, an engineer. Consider, they say, the field of basic research where scientists are working for the discovery of they know not what. They are not looking for anything in particular, and they may not find anything for years and years. How can anyone possibly measure the performance of such people?

Sometimes it appears to be impossible to set up standards of performance in terms of actual results to be attained. It *is* possible, however, to set up standards for the actions taken in an attempt to accomplish results. If we cannot say what a man should accomplish, we *can* say what a man should do to accomplish something.

There can be standards for the following: the organization of a project; the preparation of a prospectus; the time put in; the administration of the money spent and ways to account for it; the competency of personnel; the adequacy of facilities used; the modernness and utilization of equipment available; the frequency and content of periodic progress reports; the evaluation of progress; the working climate; and the like.

In other words, if we cannot measure a man's work, we can measure how he goes about his work. The assumption is, then, that if he goes about his work in the right way and nothing good comes of it, at least everything has been done that could have been done. It is tragic, however, to find that time, money, and human effort have been unintelligently expended and that results might have been attained if different approaches had been used.

There can be standards for all, therefore, and these standards can be either standards of work output or standards of work method and procedure. Quite often they can be both. We urge, however, that no one jump too quickly to the conclusion that standards of output are not possible.

1+1 Could=0

THE PRIVATE ENTERPRISE SYSTEM IS A PROFIT and loss system. If an enterprise makes a profit over a continuing period of time, it lives. If it loses money for appreciable periods, it dies. The thermometer of private enterprise is, therefore, net income and net outgo.

The key to profit is volume of sales. A certain amount of a product or service must be sold to meet fixed expense. Beyond that point, if the cost of making the product is less than the selling price, sales contribute to profit. The greater the sales, therefore, the greater the profit.

The higher the profit, the higher the income of all employees, the bigger the dividends to stockholders, the better the standard of living of consumers as more products and services are made available to more people.

The components of sales volume are quality and price. To maintain them on a small scale takes *technical know-how*; on a large scale, *management competence*. To bake a better pie than anyone in the community and get it to a neighbor fresh, unbroken, and at an acceptable price requires technical skill. To bake a thousand pies and get them to a thousand neighbors fresh, delicious, unbroken, and acceptably priced takes management skill.

Years ago, an uncle of mine had a great idea. He opened a doughnut shop. His motto was, "All the doughnuts you can eat and all the coffee you can drink for 15c." He had the windows half full of doughnuts which were sold by the dozen. His doughnuts and coffee were so good that people lined up for more than a block to buy them. His shop was open twelve hours a day and he made money fast and furiously.

Uncle Bob knew how to make doughnuts and coffee of a quality and at a price that gave him high volume and profits. He had great technical ability. "Hm," said Uncle Bob. "If one shop does so well, why not have two?" So he opened another shop uptown.

My uncle opened the second shop completely unaware of the fact that something was needed to run two shops that was not needed to run one—management ability. He personally could not give to either shop what he had given previously to one. Even if he could find two men with as much technical skill as he had, they would not have his motivation to maintain high quality and low cost. He couldn't do it! Quality went down, costs went up, and Uncle Bob went broke.

In this case, one shop plus one more shop equaled no shops.

To cook one meal, assemble one automobile, make one refrigerator, make one pair of shoes; to write one insurance policy, handle one bank account, fly one plane, or run one train takes technical know-how. To do thousands of each and maintain the same quality of product or service at a lower cost per unit takes management.

Management ability can be measured by the number of units that can be produced without loss of quality or cost position. Management makes monkeys out of addition tables because it can make 1+1 equal 0, 3, 4, 5, or 6.

The manufacturer of a well-known high-quality product recently advertised that it produced only a small number of units a day and that the company president considered the personal inspection of each unit his most important function. The implication was that it was against company policy to produce any more units than the president could inspect.

A situation such as this automatically limits the growth of the company to the inspection capacity of the chief executive. Any program calling for expansion would have to make allowance for at least one other person with the president's capacity to insure quality. This is a management problem, not a technical one.

When it is so well accepted that technical know-how has to be acquired by training, why is it sometimes assumed that management know-how will just show up when it is needed? The increasing emphasis on management training that is as specific, formal, organized, and subject to evaluation as technical training is gratifying. It is most timely as well.

Red and Green Lights

ONE OF THE MOST COMMON CONCERNS OF chief executives these days is how they can be sure that problems are spotted soon enough for the right people to take timely action. What are the most effective red lights to indicate the problems and green lights to be sure people are moving toward their solution?

This situation begins to become serious (in fact, does not appear much earlier) when an organization reaches a size and complexity that prevent personal contact by the president with everybody and knowledge about everything that is going on. This is when a company reaches the proportions where the president has to take off his overalls and move into the front office.

This stage in development is followed by a period of frustration that increases with growth, and faster than a knowledge or sense of controls and their administration can be acquired and applied.

An approach to the solution of this situation can be found in taking certain specific steps. The first is to set the course that the organization has to take. This means the establishment of short- and long-range objectives, the setting up of organizational goals. This activity begins to take a good deal of the attention of the chief executive as he releases his day-to-day control over operations.

During this planning phase, or in connection with planning activity, budgets are set up and perfected; plans take concise form and go into writing; hopes are rationalized; and specific means of attainment are identified.

The second step is the establishment of points of authority. This means we have to organize, establish management levels, set up policies, and delegate authority to take action, within the limits of policy, to the lowest point at which this action can be intelligently taken. All this has to be put in writing, and there are tools and devices by which it can be done quite clearly.

The third step is to set up means of measurement, out of which come variance reports. People at different levels report to appropriate levels as to how far they are off course, why, and what they are planning to do about it.

After the practices and techniques of setting objectives and policies have been established, plans formalized, organization structure that delegates authority clarified, and variance reports provided for, to keep the right people advised at the right time, the only feature left to incorporate is experience. There are times when instruments go wrong in the pilot's cabin and when only experience lets him know it and serves him well in the absence of instruments.

What we are saying here is that we should determine the directions in which we want to plan streets and roads; then we build the streets and roads; then we put red and green lights at the proper locations to tell people when to stop and when to go; then we keep traffic reports of whether the lights are in the right location, whether they are working effectively, how many accidents there are, and what action we are taking to prevent their recurrence. With all their scientific devices, however, traffic engineers become more competent with each year of experience with, and exposure to, traffic problems.

Superintelligence and exceptional competence may shorten the amount of experience and length of exposure required but cannot eliminate them. The conscious installation of orderly means of knowing what is going on will increase the value of effective application of experience and exposure to problems at hand.

Managers Must Inspect

To INSPECT IS AN INHERENT PART OF MANagement. No management job is performed completely unless adequate inspection control has been provided. Managers have no right to transfer this function to customers; they should not rely upon the customers to complain when quality of product or service is not up to standard.

A friend of mine and his wife recently went to a famous resort for a three-week vacation. The hotel at which they stayed was proud of the fact that its prices were the highest in the area and that its facilities and services justified them. Indeed, the prices were such as to lead one to expect nothing short of perfection.

Within a few days my friends discovered that they were receiving very slovenly maid service. By the time a week had passed, dust rolls were accumulating under the furniture and cobwebs were increasing in number overhead. Apparently nothing was ever moved for dusting, and there was no indication that water or vacuum cleaner was being employed anywhere in the cleaning process. Waste baskets were seldom emptied, and beds had to be remade if one was to sleep in comfort.

This situation became a matter of continual discussion between my friend and his wife. Not complainers by nature, they didn't want to make trouble. On the other hand, tips seemed to be expected by the help as a matter of course, with no relationship to the quantity or quality of work. And neither the housekeeper nor any other member of the management ever appeared to inspect the cleaning. The management had no knowledge of the quality of the work being done.

At the end of two weeks, the four-room suite had become so unbearably dirty that something had to be done, and my friends called the proprietor's attention to the condition. Then "the roof fell in," as one employee put it. Proprietor, manager, housekeeper, house boys, maids flew all over the place. The proprietor had "never seen such conditions." He was disturbed because he had not been notified earlier. My friend and his wife should have "reported it to the front office upon the first indication of undesirable service." The maid was fired, and my friends became known around the whole place as "royal stinkers." They now had the status they knew would result from complaint, which was the reason they had delayed so long.

The point of this story is that there was never at any time any inspection of the conditions by any member of management, but management was put out because the customer had not reported them. This is putting things backward. It is the managers' obligation to have an inspection and control system so that they know what conditions are without having to depend upon the recipient of poor service to complain.

There are indications these days of lack of proper inspection on production lines. Some unsatisfactory products are being delivered. There are reports of manufacturers' depending upon their dealers to put products in proper condition after they have been delivered to the customer because proper inspection at the plant either is not attainable or is too costly.

Another aspect of the inspection obligation also seems to be backward. Those whose work is inspected seem to resent it. They show a "Cheese it, the cops!" attitude. Individuals who work for salaries and wages are expected to produce quality services and products in return. Not only should they expect to have their output inspected, but they should be proud of having it inspected.

There are at least three constructive results to be expected from inspection of work: to see that the product or service meets the standards that have been set; to discover ways and means of improving the performance of those doing the work; to discover new and better ways to do the work. These are all basic management aims. If results are attained and workers are rewarded accordingly, then the inspection function certainly pays off for everyone and it is difficult to see why there is so much evasion of and objection to it.

A common cause of inspection breakdown is putting

the inspection function under the organizational control of those whose work is being inspected. When the auditor, for example, works for the bookkeeper whose books he is auditing, the chances are his audit will not be as objective as it would be if he were independent of this authority.

Inspection is not just a nice thing to do if and when time and money permit. It is a basic responsibility; it is an essential element of cost of production; it is a "must." The better the inspection by management the less the customer dissatisfaction and the greater the business and the profits therefrom.

Decision Making

LIFE IS EXCITING THESE DAYS BECAUSE HIStory is making amazingly clear what it has been developing over the centuries. A great multitude of human developments seem to be in, entering, or leaving definable and interesting periods. One of these is leadership.

Down through many early centuries the leader was clearly a dictator, an autocrat, a one-man operator who knew all the answers. He was a dynamic, determined, concentrated individual who ruled with an iron will over small groups or great multitudes of human beings.

History records all kinds of revolutions against and refusals to accept this kind of individual domination. Many of these have been bloody, some have been underground. They have been so prevalent and so effective, however, that that kind of leadership is no longer acceptable and is quickly identified as undesirable and outmoded by our society.

This violent human reaction against the single will resulted in a gradual swing over to what is popularly known as group dominance. This is based on the theory that the group knows more than any individual member of it and, if given the proper opportunity, will express itself in terms of the best interests of the members of the group.

This means that each individual loses himself in the identity of the group, obtains participation from the group, and ultimately receives from group action something better than he would have received—or even desired—as a result of his own thinking alone.

The scale has swung so far in this direction, in some cases, that the group has sometimes become a haven for incompetency. It has generated either actual "softies" or a concept that a leader must be a "softie" if he is to be a servant of the group. There are now evidences of some reaction against this group leadership approach just as there were against the single-individual approach. It is important, therefore, before we lose something that is good, that we get it into its proper perspective.

Just as one-man dictatorship is an undesirable extreme, so is a leaderless group. The truly desirable leadership situation seems to be a strong individual who is fully conscious of the value of and earnestly seeks the thinking and contributions of other people, but who has the courage to make a decision when it should be made even if it is contrary to the opinion of the group.

While the dictator consults no one and the group tries to manage itself, the more effective manager uses the group for full consultation, advice, guidance, and participation and then exercises his own best judgment. The dynamic group leader is a master of timing. There comes a time when a decision has to be made, when action has to be taken. A group will discuss forever unless somebody determines that the time has come to do something.

Consultative supervision requires brains, understanding, and skill to tap the experience and thinking of others as well as the competency and courage to move in accordance with one's own judgment when the time is right. It also requires considerable humility, human understanding, and a sense of the value of individual and group discipline, plus firmness.

Full effectiveness of that kind of leadership, which stands out clearly between the two extremes of despotism and group dominance, rests on confidence in one's own judgment. This does not mean "I am always right" or "Right or wrong, I am never in doubt." Many who stand stubbornly for their own viewpoints are only reflecting inner lack of confidence in them. Those who have all the answers and are constantly making them known are often suffering from various kinds of complexes, most commonly inferiority.

Making a decision is exercising judgment, and this is the essence of management. He who is skilled at making decisions is obviously a better manager than he who is not. To be skilled, you must understand all of the various component parts and processes that go into the making of a good decision and must be continually making decisions. Decision making is like playing golf—the more of it you do, the better you are. The more you practice, the more competent you become.

Many of us make the serious mistake of determining tomorrow's action in the light of today's conditions. We may decide, for example, not to build a new plant today because business is not good, only to find a year from today, when the plant would have been completed, that business is very good. We may be reluctant to expand our product research and development because our line and quality of merchandise are adequate in the present market only to find two years from today that we are practically out of the market.

Such errors are a reflection of lack of understanding of the scope and processes of decision making. Those in management must be constant students of the decision-making process and of its impact upon the exercise of their responsibilities. Competency in decision making is not to be found in the man who constantly wants to be identified as the decision maker. The manager who is able to get others to arrive at a decision which he thinks is right and to let it become their decision is also highly sensitive to the necessity of getting others to understand and accept the decisions that have been made.

A Different Approach

One of the most frustrating, most costly, and most common practices of top executives today is expecting managers of lower echelons to have immediate answers to any questions. As a result, officers of corporations get into far more detail than they have any business to and ask for far more reports than they have any reasonable need for—just so they will know the answers when the boss asks a question. This is multiplied in volume as you go down through the ranks.

The average business executive asks for much more information to be sent to him regularly than he can ever master, and he asks to have it in his own particular form. As a result, the same information is being prepared by the accounting and other departments in many different ways.

Each executive has his own little pet "black book" of a particular size, with a particular kind of page, and an odd number of columns. He dabbles into the operations of his subordinates far more than he ever should, simply to keep acquainted with what is going on.

Many department heads, plant superintendents, and division heads are busier gathering information than they are doing something about it. This is because they are concerned that an officer will ask something that they cannot answer.

This seems so ridiculous that the reader of these comments will probably not believe it exists in his particular situation. If he should open this up for discussion with his people, however, he might find it exists even though he does not want it to. This is a natural, built-in tendency on the part of many people.

A different approach to this problem would be for executives *not* to ask people for information on the spot, but to ask them if they can get it. Instead of a president's saying, "Jack, how much business have we done with the XYZ company during the past six months, and how is this business distributed percentagewise over our product line?" he might say, "Jack, would you please find out for me how much business . . .?"

Possibly, by consciously adopting this approach, we might get a feeling of relaxation into the organization in relation to this particular problem. We could impress our whole management team with the fact that there are certain centers of information available to people when they need them, but that all people do not have to be centers of information themselves.

There is another feature of this problem that is not always self-evident. Executives receive copies of far too many internal reports. This is explained as being for purposes of coordination, information, and integration. There is something about receiving information, however, that creates a sense of responsibility to do something about it.

You therefore find executives receiving reports that have nothing to do with their activity, thereby getting into activities that are none of their business. This is not only a waste of time but is irritating, confusing, and harmful to the welfare of the business.

Could we, instead of asking people for information that we would like to have, ask them if they would get us the information? In doing this we are assuming they do not have it, instead of expecting them to have it and creating a fear on their part that they might not have it.

With this same concept, could we take the approach also that we need not have information about which we should not, or do not want to, do anything at that particular time? If there are places where the information should be, and if we know that it is there, then we can call for it when we need it. We do not have to get it all the time just to have it in case we *might* need it.

This difference in approach to the whole matter of management information would, it seems to me, save a tremendous amount of executive time, of executive memory, of statistical work, of number and cost of forms, and of patience. Why clutter up our heads with phone numbers when it is perfectly easy to find one when we want it?

Management Enemy Number One

THE OFFICE MEMORANDUM IS PROBABLY THE most costly management tool for the little it accomplishes and the trouble it creates. An identification of it as "Management Enemy Number One," with picture and full description, should be posted on every bulletin board of every business office and plant.

Recently I was discussing with an executive a number of things that should have been done several months before, some of which had now developed into crises. In great agitation he called for his general manager and asked for an explanation. The general manager went to his own office and quickly returned with a handful of memoranda.

These memoranda, addressed to various members of the organization, contained instructions to take care of the items in question. Almost smugly the general manager put the memoranda on the chief executive's desk with an expression suggesting, "There! I *have* taken care of them." His attitude seemed to be that the writing of a memorandum had disposed of the matter.

That is the great danger of memoranda. There is some kind of feeling that when you have dictated instructions to somebody the job is done. Unfortunately people do not always do what they are instructed to do in memoranda, and frequently they are not able to without further clarification and assistance.

There is another aspect to memoranda that is a rather interesting commentary on human nature. We are inclined to speak much more harshly and dictatorially in a memorandum than face to face. It is like driving an automobile—behind the wheel we feel big and strong, in a mood to challenge other drivers and call them all sorts of names. When we sit behind our desks dictating instructions, our personalities are completely different from what they are when we are dealing with human beings in the flesh.

It is virtually impossible to cover all aspects of a problem in a memorandum. Almost invariably the memorandum is written to the wrong person, and others affected are not adequately informed. The result is friction, misunderstanding, and, many times, hard feelings. If a study were made of the amount of work that is actually accomplished satisfactorily as a result of writing a memorandum, I suspect the answer might be startling.

Think of the cost of memoranda. Begin with the paper and the printing of the form. There have to be, of course, many kinds of memoranda forms. There are intra-company, inter-company, inter-office, and departmental memoranda and memoranda by subject matter.

It is not uncommon for each individual executive to insist on forms with his name on them. Just walk into the stockroom some day and see the space that is occupied by memoranda forms waiting to be used ineffectively and to create trouble and frustration.

Given the particular form required, then think of the typewriter wear, the hours and hours of secretarial labor, the filing, the handling by messengers, and so on and so on. Just the filing cabinets, carefully guarding millions of memoranda, are a bit overwhelming in their volume. There are even warehouses with no other purpose but to be occupied by dead, ineffective, confusing memoranda.

Think of what normally happens to a memorandum. If the writer thinks it is important, he puts "Rush" on it. Every writer naturally thinks every memorandum is important—otherwise he would not write it—so all of them are labeled "Rush." Thus marked by rubber stamp or added sticker, they come to the desk of the busy executive. Memoranda that look too long to read at the moment he shoves aside. If they are short, he glances quickly at them to see the content and then distributes them in his desk drawers, arranging them according to the importance of the writer's position.

Seldom is any memorandum taken care of immediately. More commonly there have to be follow-up memoranda. In any case, weeks and months are likely to go by, because people usually do what is "hot" at the moment— and what is "hot" is a request or information they get from an individual personally as of a particular hour. Written communications are put aside.

What's the answer? Much easier than calling in a secretary and dictating a memorandum is speaking into the intercom or picking up the telephone or even walking to the other person's office. This personal approach carries more punch; it brings about a better understanding; it insures a better feeling; and in all probability it produces more immediate action.

There ought to be a national campaign against the memorandum. Surely it is a great enemy of good management.

Just a Bit Thoughtless

RESPECT FOR THE TIME OF OTHER PEOPLE wins their respect and confidence. Wasting others' time irritates them and results in the offender's being bypassed when opportunities arise. The guilty one is marked as unreliable, irresponsible, a bit thoughtless —and these qualities are not bench marks of success.

Lost money, lost possessions can be replaced, but not lost time. As with money, no one ever knows how much time he is going to have in life, but, unlike money, when it is lost it cannot be regained. Time is most precious, and normally we do not like those who thoughtlessly take it away from us.

There are thoughtless merchants who agree to deliver merchandise at a certain time and then fail to do so without notifying the customer of the change. Many a person has waited for the delivery of a product and made arrangements related to that delivery only to find that the product does not arrive on schedule and no one calls to let him know it will not.

Equally irritating is the service representative or repair man who agrees to be in your plant or home at a given time and then not only doesn't show up at the specified hour but doesn't show up on that day and maybe even not in that week. A call to discover the reason usually produces a humble apology and a promise to come "tomorrow." It would be much more thoughtful for the service department to set a realistic time in the first place and to call if it proves impossible to live up to the commitment.

There are those who agree to fulfill certain assignments, complete certain projects by a certain time—and never make it. In an effort at control, many managements have a system of progress reports so that people must record from time to time how close to schedule their work is. Of course, circumstances can arise that adequately excuse failure to complete work on time. In such cases, however, it is important to inform others who are affected. Then they are not taken unawares and caused to waste time waiting for something that is not coming when expected.

Some people have an easy way of saying "yes" to practically every request without any intention of doing what they have agreed to do. They say they will attend or even participate in certain functions and then back out at the last minute or fail to show up at all. They find it easier to say "yes" than to make the decision at that time. The reputation they acquire by failing to keep their word doesn't seem to disturb them particularly.

Then there is the person who is never on time for an appointment, never sends any message that he will be late, and frequently does not make it at all. He wastes the time not only of the person with whom he had an appointment but of others whose appointments were held up because of it. The irritation he creates starts him off with two strikes against him; sometimes it would be better if he did not show up at all.

Among the most thoughtless are chairmen of meetings who do not start, run, and end them on time. It is highly inconsiderate for a chairman not even to be present when a meeting is to begin, unless he has sent a message that he will be late and has asked someone else to take over until he arrives. To make those who are on time wait for late-comers to a meeting is just a bit thoughtless.

People soon catch on to such tactics. If meetings usually start late, people respond by coming later and later. When meetings do start on time, most participants are there on time. The service clubs are a good example. Their luncheons start and end on schedule. Members and guests know what to expect. They respect time and its value.

Another thoughtless tactic is calling meetings irregularly or quickly. Whenever a meeting is called on the day it is to be held, or even the day before, a lot of appointments have to be changed and other arrangements altered; as a result, plans are upset and time wasted. The most thoughtful staff meeting procedure is to establish them for certain definite times; a meeting that is not necessary can always be called off.

Unfortunately there seems to be a tradition in many organizations that whenever the boss calls you should drop everything and go at once. Many meetings are abandoned, customers left sitting, and others suspended in uncertainty while some timid soul runs for the boss's office. If informed of the situation, most bosses would say, "Well, call me when you're free." Few bosses want to force others to be thoughtless, but there seems to be some unwritten code that the top man can't be kept waiting. Surely the chief would rather wait than inconvenience many other people.

One of the most commonly heard requests is, "May I have five minutes of your time?" or, "Have you got a minute or two?" Invariably these minutes stretch to half an hour or an hour. "How ridiculous!" some might exclaim. "That's just an expression." That's right; it *is* just an expression—and a careless one. Compare it to the carelessness of a merchant who tells you the price of an article is ten cents and then charges fifty. In one case we call it carelessness; in the other, crookedness.

People who are the busiest and who accomplish the most are usually not time-wasters. You can depend on them. Regardless of how much they have to do, they are where they agreed to be at the time they agreed to be there. Perhaps that is why they are in such demand. Maybe they are successful because they are considerate of others and because they can be relied upon to do as they have agreed or to give plenty of notice of a change of plan.

The fellow who is always on time—what a bore! But at least he is not thoughtless and careless about the time of other people.

Costs!

THE ONE GREAT CRYING NEED OF ALL MANagement in the United States today is to lower unit costs. Why?

The first reason is that the United States is now a high-cost economy in relation to the world market. Foreign competition from the Common Market and from Japan has established this as a fact. While, in previous recessions in this country, foreign countries have built up a backlog of demand for our products, they did not do this in the recessions of 1958 and 1961. When we decided to recover from our recession, foreign markets did not help us. They were producing what they wanted and needed, at lower costs than we could achieve and, in many instances, with higher quality.

Our labor costs are higher; our administrative overhead is higher; and we are now popularizing what has become known as a "profitless economy." Socialistic concepts, unqualifiedly promoted by theorists in positions of power, are having a greater impact upon the public opinion of this nation than we are ready to admit. The economy of the United States is fighting for survival in the world market, and our front line of defense is costs.

Reduction of cost requires formal, specific, well-recognized, and forcefully administered cost controls. Managers at all levels must accept the responsibility for cost control that is passed on to them from above, and they must exercise stringent cost control over those below. There can be no delay nor compromise.

Management at all levels must be trained in cost control, the nature of it, and how to administer it. Managers in all categories must understand that there are automatic controls and there are measurements that indicate the necessity for exercising controls.

Never before in the history of this nation has there been such a need for conscious, specific, and immediate decisions relating to the reduction of costs. We must make decisions more quickly to move ahead with profitable items fast and without reservation. Decisions must be made to abandon many loss items immediately.

Cost-consciousness, cost reduction, cost control are not results of wishful thinking. They come only from dynamic, uncompromising, unemotional management decision. When quality is being sacrificed to cost, our position in domestic and world markets is one of diminishing return, and that is right where we are now in many product lines.

Individuals, corporations, and the nation must give primary attention to the reduction of unit costs if this nation and the civilization it represents are to survive.

Compensation Confusion

WHILE NOT PLEASANT, IT IS INTERESTING TO ponder how compensation and work have become increasingly separated over the past thirty years. There was a time when the value of what a person did and the way in which he or she did it were the basis for determining how much money a person should make and the benefits he or she should receive.

A very common philosophy today is that the compensation one receives is his share of something which is to be distributed and which is provided for all people. The main effort, therefore, is to increase one's share of it. This is, of course, a product of the welfare state.

So far as pay is concerned, the major effort seems to be to get it as high as possible through all kinds of means, while doing less and less in return for it. So far as benefits are concerned, these are primarily paid to people when they do not work. Pensions, unemployment insurance, sick leaves, vacations, paid holidays, accident benefits, all are received when one is not working. One does not object to this, but it must be pointed out that work is becoming a less and less significant factor in relation to pay and benefits.

During World War II, I held an administrative position in one of the war agencies in Washington. One morning, my secretary gleefully greeted me with the news that she had received a new title and a raise in pay. It seems that another Federal agency, established to handle personnel actions, had passed upon an application for upgrading her work and for raising her pay without any consideration by her or by them that I, as the supervisor of her work, had anything whatever to do with it. Even the fact that she was going right on doing the same work she always had been doing did not seem to impress anybody. This was a clear case of mechanical segregation of income from performance.

It used to be that compensation had a particular purpose. The kind and method of compensation influenced the attainment of certain objectives. One frequently hears questions raised in management circles similar to these: How can one make employees job-performance- and ownership-conscious? How can they be made to feel that their work is of value, that the way in which they do it provides the income with which compensation is paid, and that the real purpose of a business is to become strong and perpetuate itself in order that it may continue to make and render products and services of value to the community?

There is a formula that might be helpful and might clear up some of the confusion if one wishes to do so. It runs something like this: Base salary, pensions, and other "benefits" are paid for work done satisfactorily. If work is done as it should be done and up to standard, it has a certain value. This value should be paid as regular income and enough set aside to provide continuing income during justified time off and after retirement. *This is all in reward for doing a particular job well.*

It is natural, however, that some people should want a little extra put into a job. There are those who like to do work better than they are expected to do it, and there are managers who expend every effort to enjoy such surprises. They expect people to do more than they are called upon to do. Incentive compensation is paid for this "plus effort" and extra accomplishment over and above the requirements of the job. Bonuses, special commissions, deferred compensation—all these are for more than satisfactory work. In order that people may feel ownership-conscious—feel a pride in the business and an interest in its welfare and perpetuation—we have profit-sharing, stock purchase, and stock option plans.

Any individual who wishes to progress with satisfaction in life should not seek a position whose rewards are related to what can be obtained from influence and pressure. It is far more gratifying to be rewarded for superior performance and performance beyond the line of duty.

When compensation is considered as something that one goes after through special effort other than on the job, the issue becomes confusing. So long, however, as compensation is connected with the success and the failure of the business, it is difficult for one to provide excess incentive.

There are those who are saying today that maybe we are too liberal in our incentive plans. Maybe stock options are not having the desired effect. When such doubts are investigated, it is usually discovered that the close tie-in beween job performance and compensation, incentives, and benefits has been lost.

To Win or Not to Win

At the AMA mid-winter personnel conference in Chicago in February 1960, Bill Veeck, the president of the White Sox Baseball Club of Chicago, said, "I do not think that winning is the most important thing. I think winning is the *only* thing." During his talk, he made it perfectly clear that he wanted no part of winning at any cost or by unfair or dishonest means. He was most forceful in stating his absolute unwillingness to accept anything other than first place when the game is played in accordance with the accepted rules.

A rather common expression is, "We had a moral victory, at least." These are the words of the loser trying to rationalize and live with his loss. Never have I heard of a moral victory being anyone's objective. Attainment of such a victory, therefore, is no victory at all. It is defeat in that the objective was not attained.

The most beneficial training that I received from any part of my formal education came from varsity debating, both as a participant and as a coach. As we traveled across the country and abroad to debate colleges and universities, chapels and auditoriums were filled to overflowing. When we were away from home, we would seek out a telegraph office immediately after a contest to wire the results back to our school. The next day this telegram would be read in chapel to an enthusiastic response for a victory and moans for a defeat.

Creeping into debating circles at that time was a movement favoring the no-decision contest. The proponents of this idea came largely from among those who could not win. The plea for no-decision debating, which sometimes became quite violent, usually found mediocrity as its supporter.

It was said that debating for a decision led to intellectual dishonesty. It was believed that there was something unethical about individuals who could debate opposite sides of the same question on succeeding nights and win both debates. There were those who believed it could not be done by fair means.

The two other members of the debate team on which I served during my senior year in college were Arthur S. Flemming and F. Gerald Ensley. The former is currently president of the University of Oregon, the latter a bishop of the Methodist Church. I am sure that in the thirty years since those debating days the intellectual integrity of these men has not been questioned.

Those who doubted the reasonableness of a debating team's taking two sides of a question on different nights obviously did not believe in the old-time truth that there are two sides to every question. There isn't any position on important public issues that is all wrong. There is some good in everything.

Before completing my debating career, I was called upon to participate in two or three no-decision contests. Few experiences in my life have been so unsatisfactory and flat. It was obvious that neither team worked as hard in its preparation and neither performed as well as when a winner was to be chosen.

Striving for victory is essential for bringing out the best there is within the best. It also brings out the bad in those who are not competent enough to win by fair means. In a free system that permits the development of the best, freedom also exists for expression of the worst.

Now that no-decision debating is prevalent throughout the country, where is debating? How many consider the training they now receive as valuable? How much do you hear about it? How large are the crowds that no-decision debating draws? Where is the victory? What is the purpose?

Remember, if you will, the days and hours spent in skull practice, drill, and scrimmage with the football squad. Can you visualize yourself going through what you did, and trying as hard as you did, if no team were ever to be declared the winner? Many people today have vivid recollections of the Korean War. Many who participated in it feel that no decision was ever reached in relation to it. There was no clean-cut military victory. Maybe this has some bearing on the extremely low morale which existed among some of the troops and war prisoners and is recorded in official reports of the Defense Department.

In business, or for that matter in any organization, the making of a profit, a net, or whatever you may call it over a continuing period of time is victory. It may be noble to say that we are not in business to make a profit, but if we do not make a profit, we're not in business.

Sure, profit can be made by crooked means, but this is not success. This is not a victory because ultimately those who make a profit by crooked means go down to failure and disgrace before the inevitable judgment of society. The crooked business man is no more acceptable to the public than the dirty player.

The incentive to win is still a great incentive, particularly when a special reward goes with winning. It still brings out the best in people, both in their preparation and their performance. It is still a source of great pride and high morale to belong to a winning team or to be identified with a winning player.

Certainly there is no disgrace in not winning when one has put forth his best effort. There is nothing to be ashamed of in second or last place if one has done as well as he can. While there is no disgrace, neither is there the gratification that goes with success.

It is no disgrace to fail in one's job if one has done his best. There is no substitute, however, for having done a job well enough to be considered the best. There is no dishonor that goes with an honest failure in business, but neither is there the terrific thrill of having succeeded against great odds.

Despite all the arguments to the contrary, there is still nothing that succeeds like success. There is still nothing that brings out the best in people like winning. While there is comfort to be gained from doing one's best, there is little comfort to be gained from being second best.

Sensitivity and Gadgets

Some of the most commonly asked questions today in management circles are: How do you know? How do you know that a man knows his business? How do you know this particular person is a qualified expert? How do you know that a manager's appraisal of his subordinates is accurate? How do you know your research and development dollars are well spent?

And so we could go on and on. If a manager is not a qualified and trained expert in a given subject area and if technical devices and instruments are not available to make accurate measurements for him, isn't this a cause for much frustration?

Such questions usually are asked by managers who have not had much experience in or exposure to the activity whose measurement they are questioning. Know-how comes from exposure and experience.

Years ago, when I was in training for the oil business, part of my program was a brief experience in the oil fields. I remember one instance very vividly. A group of young engineers arrived at a certain rig with a number of imposing instruments. With these instruments they began to examine what the drill was doing, the kind of soil it was in, its depth, etc.

An old-timer, with more than thirty years of experience with drilling rigs, was both puzzled and amused as he watched the "gadgets" these young, inexperienced engineers were using to get certain information. He finally asked them what they were trying to find out. He then put his hand on the drill pipe for a few moments and told them what they wanted to know.

These younger, inexperienced men needed gadgets to find out what experienced people know almost by instinct. The answer, therefore, to many of the "how do you know" questions is that when you acquire experience of and exposure enough to an activity, you will know.

When General Brehon Somervell became president of the Koppers Company, one of his friends asked: "General, how can you head up a coke business? You don't know anything about the coke business. How can you tell whether these experts and engineers know what they are talking about? Your whole background is military." General Somervell's reply was, "I can't lay an egg, but I can smell a rotten one."

You do not have to be a doctor to know whether you have a good one. The more exposure you have to doctors, the more you develop something inside you that enables you to say, "This is a good doctor." You do not have to be able to fly an airplane to know that you have a good pilot—if you have flown enough. The more experience you have with flying, the more you are able to exercise judgment as to the competency of the pilot. You do not have to be able to bake a pie to know you are eating a good one, and the more experience you have with eating pies, the more competent you are to judge the culinary art.

If you have had a sufficient amount of experience in reviewing with your key executives their inventories of personnel, you know, without any gadgets, when they are giving you a good inventory. If, on five different occasions, you and one of your managers have reviewed his people, his appraisal of them, his plans for them, and his development program for them, you will have a certain confidence in your judgment of what he is telling you. When you have done this twenty-five times, you will have an ability along this line that you can now hardly imagine.

If you have had five experiences in reviewing with your key people their budget recommendations, you will have a certain degree of competence in determining whether they are overly conservative or too optimistic. You will have a certain amount of assurance that you are judging their problems reasonably well. When, however, you have done this twenty-five times, you will have far greater skill and competence as well as added confidence in yourself.

When, therefore, some new experience is suggested in the field of management practices, do not be concerned at first as to how you can guarantee accuracy of judgment in relation to it. Do not be too quick to seek out instruments and gadgets and procedures to insure proper evaluation. Wait a little while to see what experience with and exposure to such practice develops in the way of competence on your part to exercise fairly reliable judgment.

PART SIX

A Question of Ideas

There is no adequate defense, except stupidity, against the impact of a new idea.

P. W. Bridgman
The Intelligent Individual and Society

Idea Prospecting

The gold prospector pans tons of gravel, dirt, and sand over a period of time in the hope of finding a few nuggets of precious metal. Only upon very rare occasions can gold be found without sifting great quantities of earth.

So it is with valuable ideas. Great quantities of words must be uttered if a few priceless ones are to be discovered. Unless we read volumes and listen to days and weeks of discussion, our search for valuable thoughts is much less likely to be productive.

Complaint about meetings is common. The strong silent type despises them; the shallow mentality avoids them; the tongue that wags at both ends loves them. There is much that is lost, however, without them.

It is impossible for competent people to gather in a meeting for the purpose of exchanging ideas under capable leadership without ideas being sparked that otherwise might never have come into being. Meetings are commonly thought of as media of communication, but they are also creative. That individual who maintains he gets nothing out of a meeting probably never actually participated in one. He may have been physically present, but his mind must have been somewhere else or nowhere at all.

Talk, talk, and more talk—that is the stuff of which ideas are made. It is the gravel and the sand that pass through the prospector's pan. If he is persistent, intent, and observant, then the more he sifts the more nuggets he will find.

There are prospectors for gold, of course, who spend much time working where there is none. No matter how diligently they search, they cannot find nuggets where there is no gold. So it is with anyone who seeks ideas. He will find them at meetings only if the people gathered there have the kind of background and experience that, when presented, exchanged, and discussed, bear upon the problem to be solved or the area of creativity desired.

Recently it was my privilege to participate in a demonstration of "brainstorming." In approximately six minutes twenty-five men, separated into groups of five each, came up with thirty-eight suggestions for solving a specific problem that had been presented. Here was a great volume of talk produced in a brief amount of time. Much was irrelevant, and some was most impractical.

There were, however, some real nuggets. There were two or three very specific ideas that were clearly stated, and there were half a dozen more suggested by the overtone of the whole list. These will be put to good use. Out of that six minutes of chatter have come some ideas that undoubtedly will pay off in some thoroughly tangible practices over the next twelve months.

If this same group had been permitted to pursue this technique for six hours, there is no question that a perfect gold mine of constructive ideas would have emerged. Idea prospecting requires a lot of talk, either orally or in writing, from people who have something to contribute to the type of ideas sought, combined with some careful screening to search out the intellectual gems. This is as thrilling an occupation and gets as deeply into one's blood as gold prospecting. If, however, one goes through life bored by the sound of others' voices, hypnotized by his own silence, unwilling to concede that anybody has an idea which will help another or inspire a new idea in another, he will not find this point of view acceptable.

It is undeniable that a good deal of idle, useless chatter; dangerous, time-consuming, harmful gossip; misconceptions; insinuations; half-truths; and untruths flows out of human mouths. There are murderous, character-slashing words and comments. That is true, however, of almost anything in a free society.

Under a system that permits the highest possible degree of goodness, badness is also possible. Where the highest possible development in human character and potential can take place, there too you can find the lowest form of human existence. Where profit can be made fairly and on a high plane it also can be made by crooked means. A surgeon's scalpel that can save a life can also cut a throat.

The fact that evil use of a human talent is possible does not mean that prohibition of its use is wise. The presence of cinders, shale, cactus, and other forms of rubble in the prospector's gravel is no reason for him to cease his search for gold. Tons of dirt have produced ounces of precious metal. Mountains of talk may have similar value—"Thar's gold in them thar hills."

Most Expressed Need

FRUSTRATION IS EXPERIENCED BY TOO MANY management people today. The major cause of it seems to be others' lack of recognition of their ideas and activities.

Managers become frustrated because they have not obtained or cannot obtain understanding and cooperation from other segments of the organization. Scientists often feel that the marketing and manufacturing people do not appreciate what they are doing and even consider research and development unnecessary overhead. Personnel executives sometimes think their activities are merely tolerated by others. The production man is frequently under the impression he is being kicked around by those who are trying to squeeze more out of costs while demanding more quality.

The insurance administrator is taken too much for granted and cannot get enough people to listen to what he is doing and to its importance. The packaging engineer, who is dealing with one of the most costly and significant activities in a business, frequently cannot get a hearing. The office manager seems to be so much a part of the family that few realize what would happen if we suddenly did not have him. The financial executive is quite sure no one else in the organization understands the value of a nickel.

It is interesting that the least frustration of this kind seems to exist among marketers. Seldom do you hear this kind of complaint from a salesman. If anything, other executives complain that marketers get too much attention and consideration from others and that they are frequently recognized more liberally in the pay envelope. Perhaps this situation is worthy of some analysis.

Some of these frustrations (because of inability or lack of opportunity to win the attention, interest, and cooperation of others) may arise from lack of skill in the making of presentations. There certainly are great differences in the quality of presentations. It is a fact that the need most commonly expressed by managers is for help on how to present ideas, information, facts, and programs to others.

During a recent discussion of this problem the following observation was made by an executive in the group: "Marketers make a presentation with charts, colored slides, drama, proper emphasis, and oratorical skill while a scientist frequently stumbles along sneaking an occasional glance at a scrap of paper in the palm of his hand." It is possible that marketers are less frustrated by inability to influence others because they are more skilled in the making of quality presentations.

Some try to overcome this handicap by taking

courses in public speaking. There is some thought that the orator is more effective than those who cannot express themselves ably. This is all to the good, but it is not the whole story. Effectiveness of presentation includes much more than the public speaking factor, and many presentations are quite effective without much speech skill. What are some of the elements involved in good presentations?

The first requisite is clear-cut, written identification of the problem or idea or program to be presented. A positive print can be no better than the negative from which it is printed. No idea can be transmitted to another mind any more clearly than it exists in the mind of the presenter.

The second factor is careful organization of the presentation. Major and minor points must be identified. The thoughts and the information and the points to be put across must be organized in a specific outline. It is necessary to decide how many major premises have to be established and, for each of the major premises, how many minor premises and, for each of the minor ones, how many subminor. There has to be balance so that detail will not smother more important issues.

Third, very careful consideration must be given to the best possible visual aids to support the presentation. Charts, graphs, slides, movies, recordings, and the like all have vital uses, but if they are used too much at the wrong times and with improper emphasis, the result can be very boring.

Careful consideration must be given to the background, the time, and the interests of the audience. Each presentation must be adapted to the particular listener or listeners. A minor point for one group may become a major point for another—and vice versa.

In the fifth place, there must be great sensitivity to audience reactions as a presentation is progressing. Some listeners grasp a point much more quickly than others. When that is evident, there is no use driving an idea into the ground. Parts of presentations must be left out and others elaborated on to meet the situation.

Many other factors in presenting one's own ideas and information to other people might be discussed. The only reason for stating any of them is to make it clear that managers' frustrations could be greatly reduced if more careful attention were given by individual managers to the development of specific presentations.

When someone makes no effort to gain the understanding and cooperation of others, he has no right to complain about not having them. One has no right to expect any better response from others than the quality of his presentation justifies. Help in this area is today's most expressed need among managers.

You Can't Lose

ONE CANNOT SPEND MONEY, TIME, EFFORT, or thought without getting something in return. The quantity and quality of the return are dependent upon the individual's determination of the return desired, his concentration upon securing it, and the environment in which it is sought.

When a man loses a dollar bill, he at least receives a lesson on carelessness. If he squanders it, he has the pleasure of doing so. If he buys a necktie with it, he has filled a material need. If he pays it out for food, he has met a necessity. If he invests it, he may increase it. If he places it in his church's collection plate, he has met a responsibility. So it is with time, effort, and thought!

One of the most common complaints heard in management circles today concerns time spent in meetings. "We spend so much time in meetings that we do not have time to run the business." "You go to the meetings, and I'll tend store." "If we have all these meetings, who is going to make the profits?"

All action is preceded by thought. The nature of

action, therefore, is determined by the kind of thinking that has preceded it. Thinking in a vacuum produces more than no thought at all, but thought stimulated by others produces greater return.

It is impossible to think with others, or to listen to others' thoughts, without getting something out of it. What one gets depends upon what he wants, how he concentrates on getting it, and the people with whom, and the conditions in which, he does his thinking. You can't lose!

Even if a person is not paying attention to what is being discussed in his presence, his mind is not blank. It may wander; it may dream; but it is never inactive, even when one sleeps. While the quality of the mental product reflects this, there is a product.

Some are inclined to observe that because an individual leaves a discussion with the same opinions or ideas with which he entered it, the "thinking together" has contributed nothing to him. This cannot be. He at least is further convinced of the rightness of his own position. He has acquired deeper convictions. He cannot lose!

To have time to think is important in one's activity. To have the opportunity to be exposed to the stimulation of the thinking of other people is precious. To make the most of it, give consideration to what you hope to get out of thought; concentrate on getting it; and give careful attention to the environment in which you seek it.

The next time you are in a meeting, let observations

such as the following pass through your mind: "How fortunate I am to have this time to think! How fortunate I am to have other minds available to think with! How can I make the most of this opportunity?" The result will have an impact upon your action. Maybe you will tend the store better. Maybe you will make more profit more readily. You can't lose.

Put It in Writing

THE PRACTICE OF PUTTING IMPORTANT MATTERS in writing is growing rapidly; in fact, it is an overwhelming trend. Plans, policies, position descriptions, standards of performance, progress reviews are going down on paper.

There are still those who cry out in pain over the invasion of the privacy of one's mind, or of the board of directors' room. It is a losing battle. Communication is the order of the day. It is the greatest skill, the most important skill, and the hardest to master.

The firm foundation upon which good communication is built is clarification of thought. Before thought can be transmitted effectively, it must be clear. A poor print can be made from a good negative, but a good print never can be made from a poor negative.

Writing is the most effective means I know for clarifying thought. It is effective not only for clarifying the thought of an individual, but also for clarifying the thoughts of a group.

If you really want a group to contribute to thought, if you want the group to develop something better than any individual member of it could have developed alone, then let the group see what they are developing. Put on a blackboard, or type, reproduce, and bring back to the group for observation and study, what is being said.

By this means the members are consciously creating, arranging, establishing, and relating thoughts. They are molding them before their own eyes. If they cannot see what they are producing, they wander off in different directions; they repeat; they waste time; they make little progress.

If an individual has a sincere, deep yearning to clarify his own thinking, there is no better way to do it than to put it in writing. He who would shape words into clear thoughts is no different from the artist who paints a picture on canvas, a sculptor who chisels marble, an architect who draws an elevation of a finished building, or an engineer who drafts a blueprint. With paper before him and pencil or pen, a thinker is a creative artist with his tools at hand.

A manager who has clarified a policy and put it in writing receives the same satisfactions from the feedback of the understanding of people who read it that an artist receives from watching people interpret his painting in a gallery. A manager who develops a practical, sound, long-range plan and with the help of appropriate people reduces it to intelligible form receives the same thrill of attainment when his people buckle down to the task as does the orchestra leader with the musicians responding to his fingertips.

There is very little real comprehension of the lack of understanding of the spoken word. In the first place, people do not hear what is said. Either they do not listen, or they do not want to hear, or they do not understand, or the understanding that they get is based upon a different background of experience. So far as I know, no one has yet reduced to any understandable form the extent of myriad meanings to different people of the same words. One simple little word can have as many different meanings as there are people who hear it and understand it their way.

Putting thoughts in writing causes one to give greater consideration to what words look like and mean. Putting these thoughts in writing with the help of other people insures greater understanding by those people of the meaning of the words.

Putting it in writing means greater assurance of its understanding and attainment. Putting it in writing is a requisite of good communication. Putting it in writing is an art, and the manager who consciously tries to put in writing something that has been created within his own mind is an artist and receives the gratifications that go with successful art.

Thought Provokers

TOOLS ARE INTENDED TO AUGMENT SKILL. UNfortunately the tool frequently receives greater emphasis and overshadows the skill it augments.

There are many aids that assist mental skill. It is not at all uncommon, however, for the aid to become so glorified that any use of the mind is overlooked. The tools for aiding the exercise of judgment often have their greatest significance in the fact that they are thought provokers. They make people do thinking that they otherwise would not do, and therefore the result of the thinking is better.

The marvel and drama of the electronic business machine frequently cause us to overlook completely what this machine does for mental skill. Before the machine is ever used, before it is ever installed, it has already brought about some of its greatest benefits in that the preparation for its use has forced an examination and reorganization of what we are doing. The machine does not in itself improve the paperwork so much as it causes thought that improves procedure. In other words, the mere anticipation of the tool provokes thought that otherwise would not even be exercised.

In discussing organization structure, we frequently use organization charts, position descriptions, activity analyses, work-flow charts, and other tools for clarifying responsibility and authority. Often these techniques get blown up out of all proportion as compared with the importance of the thinking processes they generate. An attempt to clarify the functions and relationships of people within a group necessitates thought that otherwise would not take place. The position description, therefore, does not clarify organization so much as it clarifies thought. The thought is better because of the use of the tool.

Research devices and procedures do not derive their primary importance from what they produce in themselves. These research techniques bring attention to bear upon a given subject matter and provoke thought that makes the discovery or arrives at the conclusion. There is no better illustration of this today than the satellites that are now encircling the earth. Undue importance has been given to the satellites as such, and the necessity for getting them into their orbits has been much overemphasized. The greatest value of the program is not in the satellites themselves but in the discoveries that have resulted and will result from the attempt to get them into space.

Many times people will argue and even become irritated over differences of opinion as to the acceptability of a certain performance standard. There seems to be an impression that if the standard is not perfect, then it will not accomplish what it is supposed to accomplish. There is, in my opinion, only one result a standard is supposed to accomplish and that is to generate thought processes which develop a clearer concept of what constitutes a job well done.

The tool that is used as an aid to mental skill does not primarily do something in itself. It provokes thinking processes and the use of sharper mental skills that determine certain actions to be taken. Thus the result is attained from the thought provoked and not from the tool itself.

It is important, therefore, that the tools which are primarily thought provokers do not become so important and so glorified that they diminish our consciousness of the power of the mind. Let us keep clearly in the forefront the thought that the mind becomes bigger and better and sharper because of the existence and use of the tools.

The electronic computer forces the mind to work as it has never worked before, to identify and make decisions under pressure, to analyze and evaluate various avenues of approach to given problems. If there ever was a thought provoker, it is to be found in this situation.

With the exception of very specific, technical information required in highly specialized training, the value of education is not to be found in the knowledge acquired. In fact, much of the knowledge acquired in high school and college is lost long before it could possibly be of any practical use.

The greatest value of formal education is the training

of the mind. The more the mind is provoked to work and the more it is directed in orderly processes, the more effective it becomes. There is little difference between physical training and mental training as to the nature of the result. A body that is constantly in training is better able to measure up to supreme requirements when called upon. The more the mind is trained, the sharper it is and the more ready it is to meet the challenges of the times and circumstances in which it finds itself.

It may be provoking to have to follow periodic exercise routines to avoid or reduce increasing flabbiness of the physical being. Similarly, it could be provoking to have to challenge the mind and exercise it to keep it from being lethargic. Nothing, however, is of great value unless it is the result of considerable effort. Effort is, in turn, a product of great personal strength and discipline.

No Substitute

THERE IS NO SUBSTITUTE FOR THE HUMAN mind. Surely there is no greater creation on the face of this earth. No force contains so much, can do so much, or has so great a potential.

There are many aids to the mind. Information, experience, knowledge, personal guides, and many other such influences have a profound effect upon it. Many mechanical devices, techniques, and methods assist the mind in its exercise of judgment and in its intricate movements.

That mind which closes itself to aids, information, and guides is less powerful and less effective than the mind which makes judicious and wise use of what is available to it. That mind which accepts substitutes for its own workings and refuses to exercise its own judgment is just as limited and impotent.

It is not uncommon today to hear references to powerful and awe-inspiring new electronic business machines that "think." There is a misconception among some that they will be a substitute for mental brilliance and, therefore, that minds may become less significant in the future. But even to speak of a computer as an "electronic brain" is a great mistake. There is not today and there never will be a bloodless machine that can think. What these machines do and will do is to give the human mind such assistance as it has never before enjoyed or even conceived, and they will, therefore, challenge it to greater and greater attainment.

Electronic business machines can supply us with facts and information never before available. Minds that previously were occupied in the accumulation of certain data, which now are provided mechanically, are being relieved of that function, leaving them free to think about those data.

Many seem to believe that various batteries of personnel tests are substitutes for judgment. There are executives and companies that accept the findings of such devices. It would seem that there have been enough catastrophes from such practices to have taught us a lesson, but the need to learn over and over again for our own personal satisfaction is a human characteristic.

Personnel tests are a valuable aid to the exercise of our judgment about people, but whenever they become a substitute for judgment, we have mechanized our thinking and are permitting our mental powers to shrivel.

Exercise and practice are good for the mind and improve judgment. Occasionally one hears the comment that a person or a number of persons gained nothing from attendance at some conference, seminar, course, or other meeting. This usually means that he or they did not go home with a single suggestion or idea that was of specific use in a particular situation.

An individual who admits having received no help from pertinent presentations or discussions by others is saying, in essence, that his mind did not function while he was present. Even if no specific idea was obtained from another, it seems incredible that the ideas of others should not have sparked thoughts that otherwise might not have occurred to the listener or participant. This is what we mean when we say that a certain experience has been thought-provoking.

It is not possible for an active business executive to sit for a period of hours, days, or weeks doing nothing but thinking about his job and how he does it without improving his job performance. He is devoting time to thought, aided by others, and this thought results in judgment that he could not otherwise have had.

The use of the many aids that are now becoming available causes the mind to be used more frequently and more rapidly, which increases practice in the use of judgment. Great and numerous as are all the aids to judgment, however, there is no greater aid to a mind than another mind. There is no substitute. While no mind can assemble or retain all the machine-produced information, facts, and figures that appear on paper and film, only a mind can interpret, inspire, and enthuse. Only a mind can make the all-important decisions.

What is more valuable than judgment, which is a

product of the mind? Judgment is also a reflection of the soul and spirit of a human being, but these in turn are influenced by the mind and reflected through it. Those aids and influences that improve the capacity and the deliberations of the mind are, therefore, extremely valuable.

When we think of the systems, devices, and machines that are accomplishing great things in the realm of information and analysis, we must always remember that they are enhancing the power of the mind, not minimizing its importance. There is no substitute for the mind. There is simply a greater challenge each day that requires increasing capacity and quality of mental deliberation.

PART SEVEN

The Development Process

A man who qualifies himself well for his calling, never fails of employment.

Thomas Jefferson
Writings

It's More Difficult

There are many questions these days as to why all the interest in and attention to management development. Twenty-five years ago it was considered improper even to use the terms "management training" and "manager development" because it was assumed that when a man became a manager he knew enough and had the skills required to do the job. Today hundreds of thousands of managers are attending formal courses in our universities, at professional societies, and within their own companies.

The most common answer given to the question about all this activity is that the management job is growing more complex. It is said to be more complex because it is larger; it is subject to many more outside pressures and regulations; its obligations are more commonly understood; and the ethics of management are so much higher that there is greater personal concern about living up to the standards established.

One of the greatest reasons, however, why the job of the manager is more difficult today than a quarter of a century ago is that no one person is capable of making all the decisions required. This means that the modern manager must rely upon the judgment of others. It is easier to exercise one's own judgment than it is to obtain, evaluate, and have confidence in the judgment of other people.

The average person has much more confidence in his own judgment than he has in the judgment of someone else—even when he knows the other person is more qualified to exercise that judgment. He feels more secure in his own judgment because at least he knows how he arrived at his opinion and he is not sure what processes the other person went through.

We talk today about the shift from the autocratic, one-man type of operation to the democratic, consultative type of supervision. What we are talking about is the person who exercises judgment versus the person who gets others to exercise judgment. We talk about centralization versus decentralization. What we are referring to is having all the decisions made in one place versus having them made at many places by people in much better positions to make them.

This shift from exercising one's own judgment to selecting and developing those who can exercise judgment is real and dramatic. It is no longer a matter of choice. A manager either makes this shift or goes down to defeat.

This, therefore, is in my opinion one of the factors contributing to all the current interest in management development. More and more managers today are concerned with how to find people who can make good decisions than they are with making decisions themselves. No one is born with good judgment. It is acquired through the accumulation of know-how, practice, and experience.

Know-how, practice, and experience normally come with the years. That is why judgment usually improves with age and maturity. This process, however, can be speeded up. Practice may be intensified by stringent periods of programed and supervised drill. Experience can be attained through conscious, concentrated exchange with other people engaged in the area of experience desired. Know-how can be greatly enlarged through well-known scientific educational processes.

These are the basic purposes of management development. When we speak of courses, conferences, seminars, clinics, and round tables, we are identifying carefully prepared and directed media for supplying a background for good judgment more rapidly than if the development of the modern manager were left to time and chance.

Measuring Managers

There is much curiosity, discussion, and research about methods for determining how good a manager really is. "How can a manager be measured?" is a question frequently heard in management circles.

Personal productivity can be measured, but to judge a manager upon that alone ignores the basic definition of management, that it is getting things done through other people. The sales made by a sales manager, the output a foreman gets from a machine, the batting and fielding averages of a baseball team's playing manager are not measurements of managerial effectiveness. To give much attention to them puts the emphasis in exactly the wrong place.

How about the output of the manager's subordinates? Would that not be a fair measure—if the manager's job is to get his people to attain results? In part it would be, but even that has to be analyzed. Frequently the results attained by an organization reflect conditions over which no one has control. A flood can cut plant output. A new and aggressive advertising campaign can increase sales. In neither case would the skill of immediate supervision be indicated by the figures.

There is, I believe, a way to measure how good a manager is. It is a method that has been tried in parts, but I do not know of any case where it has been tried in its entirety. In my opinion, a fair and constructive way to measure the performance of a manager is to measure the improvement shown over specific periods of time by those individuals who receive their day-to-day supervision from him.

Acceptance of this idea depends first upon acceptance of the principle that a manager's job is to develop people, to help them realize their fullest potential in character, personality, and productivity. Even though actually people are not developed but must develop themselves, it is a manager's obligation to offer full opportunity for and assistance in such development.

Acceptance of this idea depends secondly upon understanding that an individual consists of certain knowledge, skills, habits, and attitudes that can be changed. Such changes, furthermore, are greater and more favorable when they are brought about in a conscious and organized way than when they are left to chance.

Knowledge can be measured. It is necessary first to outline the information and experience a person should have to do a given job well. Then at any given time examinations can be conducted to determine how actual knowledge compares with desired knowledge. This is an old, well-known technique about which there is little question or difficulty.

The possession of a skill and the degree of excellence

in its use can be determined. When we know what skills are required to do a job, we can discover their presence in an individual by test and observation. There is nothing new or difficult about this.

Habits are identifiable and describable. Once we have listed the kinds of work habits we would like someone to exercise on his or her job, we can tell quite easily how any individual on that job measures up. Personal "off the job" habits are of interest to the manager when they affect performance on the job. These also can be identified without difficulty.

Attitudes can be ascertained and defined. What attitudes does a manager have a right to expect from his people toward job, superior, associates, company, and products? The means of finding out what people's attitudes actually are have been professionally developed and proved. This task requires expert help. It is no job for an amateur.

If the above observations are correct, then this is a way in which we can evaluate a manager: At a given time determine the knowledge, skills, habits, and attitudes of each of the individuals who report to the manager directly without intervening supervision. Compare the findings with the knowledge, skills, habits, and attitudes that are desired for each job performed by such individuals. Do the same thing one year later for the same individuals. Note the changes that have taken place. Those changes provide an accurate measure of the manager's impact (or lack of it) upon his people. Then check the performance of these same individuals. There will be a direct relationship between their development and their performance unless some factor beyond their control is reflected in the results.

Some question the amount of time it takes for managers to measure managers and for managers to measure their people, particularly as suggested here. Certainly it takes time. What better use can managers make of their time? If any other activities are interfering with a manager's evaluating and helping to develop his people, then he should get rid of those activities. That's why we have staff services.

Some point out that people do not like to be inspected and measured. We do not like many phases of life that are good for us. Many children dislike school and some of their teachers. Young people often resent chaperones. Most grownups object to many of the restrictions placed upon us by society and its institutions. Human development, however, requires certain disciplines, unpopular though they may be. We are better for them.

Individual managerial effectiveness should be determined. If a manager's job is to influence others to do what should be done, then his effectiveness can be determined by measuring his influence upon others. If he is led to think constantly of his influence upon others, he is more likely to be organized and careful about it—and thus to exert a greater and a wiser influence.

Conference Appraisal

It is interesting to note how frequently something that is originated for one purpose is evaluated as a failure in the accomplishment of another. It is obviously ridiculous to criticize a badminton court because it is not large enough for tennis. It would be even more startling for someone to observe that automobiles are inadequate because they will not fly.

It is interesting to listen to all of the shortcomings attributed to the group or conference appraisal technique, now quite commonly used as a method for evaluating the present capacities and future potential of management people. This is a system whereby three or more people appraise another in group discussion. These people are neither subordinates nor peers of the person being appraised. This approach contrasts with one person making the appraisal; one making it and two or three others separately endorsing or rejecting it; or two or three people all making separate and independent appraisals of another.

Some of the comments made about the conference appraisal system are as follows: It is the immediate supervisor's job to appraise his people, and others should not do it for him; nobody knows the individual so well as the immediate supervisor, so others cannot contribute much; there are not enough people who know the one being appraised to justify a conference; the resulting appraisal is not absolutely accurate and fair; appraisal conferences take too much time; the procedure is too complicated; etc. With these and other criticisms in mind, let us now take a look at the original purpose of the conference appraisal system.

The formal conference or group method of personnel appraisal started approximately twenty-five years ago. The soundness of it was based on such assumptions as those in the following paragraphs.

It is the basic job of a manager to get his people to produce.

One of the essential steps in getting people to produce is to advise them from time to time on how well they are producing and where opportunities for improvement lie; this requires as fair and accurate judgment of performance as it is possible to obtain.

The judgment of a supervisor will be exercised more regularly when times are established for using it.

A supervisor's judgment as to the performance of his people will be fairer and more accurate when he has to present it to other people, when his judgment is sharpened by their questions, and when adequate time is spent in arriving at it.

Arriving at accurate and fair judgment of an individual is not a simple procedure, and it takes time.

Wherein was this any improvement on previous practice? The most common procedure used up to that time—and still used by many—is as follows: The personnel department or some other staff agency periodically writes the supervisor asking him to appraise his subordinates. The supervisor is a busy man and he does not do it immediately, so the personnel department needles him until he does. When he has been needled sufficiently, he will then do it as quickly as he can—either on the train on the way home, on the kitchen table while waiting for dinner, or in the office between appointments. He then gets it off to the personnel department, and that's that.

Usually in such a procedure his purpose is to satisfy the schedule demands of a staff department rather than do a good job of appraisal. The completed form then goes into the files, and there generally is no further reference to it by the supervisor.

Furthermore, there was, and in many circles still is, an effort to simplify the appraisal procedure. Forms were developed on which the supervisor makes checkmarks in arriving at what he believes to be an appropriate profile of the individual being appraised. He usually can do this in five or ten minutes. The form then goes to some expert who places a key over it and comes up with a mathematical computation that tells how good the individual is, or how good his performance is, or where he might be going.

The impact of this highly systematized, overly simplified appraisal speed-up upon the performance of individuals was very slight. It was felt, therefore, that a supervisor should take the time to appraise his people and particularly their performance.

If a date is set for a conference with others on the appraisal of his people, the manager will take the time when he otherwise might not. If the appraisal is made with and in the presence of others, he will take more time and care, and the result usually is fairer and more accurate than otherwise. It is, however, always the supervisor's appraisal.

The purposes of group appraisal, therefore, are: to see that the supervisor takes the time required when it is required; to give the supervisor all possible assistance in reviewing the performance of his people; to see that the supervisor discusses appraisals with those appraised and suggests ways and means by which they might improve. It would be very difficult to prove that it does not fulfill these purposes. Be sure what it was intended to do before judging its effectiveness.

Peer Pressure

RECENTLY, IN A DISCUSSION OF THE MAJOR problems of top executives, I heard an expression that was brand-new to me: "peer pressure." The phrase was used by Jess E. Hall, Jr., president of the Weatherford Oil Tool Company of Houston, Texas. (When questioned, he attributed it to George Corless, retired head of management development activities for the Standard Oil Company of New Jersey.) It means the impact of one's equals upon one's self.

To be tried before one's peers is a basic right under the democratic system. Human beings seem to be more sensitive to the reactions and feelings of their equals than they are to those of others. This is one of the reasons for the great value of team play as contrasted with individual play. That executive who works through and with the members of his staff in a spirit of securing their full participation in exercising his responsibilities knows exactly what this value is.

It is frequently harder for a member of an organization to sell his associates on an idea than it is to sell his boss. The evaluation of him by his peers is usually more exacting and more severe than is that of his boss.

When there is a weak member on a team, the other members of the team, if given the opportunity, will exert certain pressures upon that individual that are far greater than anything the boss can ever bring to bear. Any person who is not pulling his load will feel such pressure from the group of which he is a part, and the individual who is doing his share or more will sense the approval of his associates.

If a manager is to derive the fullest advantage from peer pressure, he must operate to some extent through group action. He will be greatly aided in forming his judgment upon an important project or program if he has the individual particularly interested in the proposal present it to a group of all those concerned rather than just to the higher manager.

Take, for example, the formulation and administration of a budget. The controller works with individual members of the staff and line in drawing up the initial budget. The chief executive then calls these individuals together and asks the controller to present the complete budget as it exists at that time to the whole group of individuals with responsibility toward it. Each individual in the group is asked to explain his accomplishments of the past year in relation to his budget and to justify any differences in budget for the coming year. Why does he think he can produce more income, and/or why does he require any increase in expense?

The budget resulting from such a procedure will be much more accurate than one formulated after the controller has discussed it with each individual singly, or even after the controller and each individual have gone over it with the chief executive. Justifying one's self before a group of one's equals is a tough job, and people do not take it lightly. They can't get away with very much, and they are forced into much more careful preparation than they would otherwise give.

An advertising program, an organization structure, a new product, a cost reduction program, a quality control effort—each will be given more careful examination by a group of the associates of the person presenting it than by the chief executive alone, and this approach will lead to a wiser decision on the part of the chief executive.

When there are goals to be attained, it is well to have individuals appear before a group to explain where they are in relation to the goals and why they are off course, if they are. In most cases these individuals will present much more accurate explanations and will receive far greater assistance from their associates than they would in any other way. This is particularly true in the area of management appraisal and development work.

The most successful programs of management development with which I have been acquainted are those that provide review boards or review committees before which key executives come to explain what they are doing in the selection, appraisal, and development of their subordinates. They identify their people and appraise them for the board or committee, and those appraisals have to be justified. Not only does this need for justification help to compel more careful advance consideration of the appraisals, but the suggestions made during the review also help to improve the ultimate result.

Committees, conferences, group discussions are not valuable simply to make people feel they are participating. One of their greatest values is the constructive pressure that the group as such puts upon each of its members to measure up—a pressure that can be equaled under no other circumstances.

Too Many Good Managers?

This is the era of management development. There has been more consideration of and more activity in manager training in the past ten years than in the entire previous history of the United States. This period in the management evolution will be recorded as the one in which management came of age as a profession.

Questions that never fail to come up in discussions about executive development programs are: "What do you do when you have more well-selected, formally trained, competent managers than you can use? What is the impact upon morale when you cannot challenge these managers with a sufficient amount of responsibility?"

Personally, I have never known a situation where such a condition actually developed. If management is functioning as it should, it seems impossible that such a condition could develop in a growth company.

A growth company is one that is progressing, both in size and in competency. Growth in this connection means that each individual in the company is growing in competency and in productivity and that the company, as a whole, also is growing in these respects.

All managements should clarify their official policy in relation to growth. Do they want to remain as they are—doing a nice, reasonable business and making a comfortable profit—or do they want to expand? If they want to expand, what direction should this expansion take—making greater sales of existing products, adding to the line with similar products, or producing completely diversified products and services? If they decide not to expand, their perpetuation is in serious jeopardy, and in all probability the company will be acquired by someone else.

If it is an accepted policy that a company wants to grow, the surest way is to increase its number of competent, well-trained people. The introduction of an appreciable number of such people at any level in the management organization upgrades that entire level. Those who can do big jobs can do lesser ones better than people who never can do more than the lesser jobs.

Development of foremen that has been left to chance, for example, usually results in a run-of-the-mill, mediocre group of individuals who have no particular desire to get anywhere. The performance of such individuals reflects this attitude. If, on the other hand, all foremen are given a chance to participate in formal training and all potential foremen have a similar opportunity, the whole foreman echelon will be more dynamic and effective in its work.

If there are individuals in first-line supervision who, through their own development, are putting pressures on the level above them and are forcing themselves up into this higher level, they will upgrade the higher level to better performance. This pressure is exerted all the way to the top and becomes so potent that it forces a company to grow and expand. Such people want opportunity, make opportunity, and will do everything in their power to find opportunity within the framework of the organization of which they are a part.

In most cases, a management that finds itself in a position of having competent people who are underutilized will find opportunities to utilize them. If challenges for such people cannot be developed within the framework of the existing organization, the management either will start new programs, new products, new services, or will go out and acquire them. Much of the current merger activity is the result of companies with inadequate managements being acquired by companies with a good supply of management talent. In many cases, the latter are looking for a place to use their management talent and to use it constructively.

It has been frequently said, and rightfully so, that no one can develop a manager—he must develop himself. One can, however, expose an individual to opportunity which will cause him to develop more than he would otherwise. Such exposure whets his appetite; sharpens his curiosity; motivates him to greater attainment.

If, therefore, an enlightened, progressive management has decided upon a growth pattern, it cannot have too many good managers. And chances are that the management that has been lulled to sleep by its own complacency also will not have too many good managers—for they will not stay with such an organization.

*Manager Training in Proper Perspective**

**Perspective: The relation of parts to one another and to the whole, in a mental view or prospect.*

IT HAS BEEN STATED ON NUMEROUS OCCASIONS that management, as a profession, is in the same position today as the medical profession was in when doctors decided that working in a drug store or helping doctors was not sufficient training to be a doctor. This means that exposure to managers or helping managers is no longer considered sufficient training to be a manager.

This is substantiated by the tremendous and dramatic growth in manager training activities and in the use of professional management techniques during the past decade. The number of managers enrolled in formal management training programs within their own companies, in universities and colleges, with management consultants, or in professional societies has grown from less than 10,000 a year in 1948 to over 600,000 in

1962. Professional management techniques, intelligently and ably used by a few isolated managers in the late 1940's, are now a matter of common practice by thousands of managers.

This fantastic growth in manager training and the resultant use of scientific management techniques have thrown many people into complete confusion as to what it is all about. There are those who think manager training is just a fad, and it is true that some aspects of it can be so classified. Many people who have no fundamental understanding of what it is are participating in it simply because it appears to be the popular thing to do.

Contributing to the confusion are those who, though obviously unqualified to speak with authority on professional management and manager training, do so nonetheless. There are also those who have an extremely limited viewpoint of professional management and who approach its attainment in a superficial and hazardous way.

In an Associated Press article appearing in the New York *Herald Tribune* on Friday, December 11, 1959, the following statement was printed:

> The leftist economic czar of Cuba, Major Ernesto Guevara, asked Cuban and foreign firms today to train military officers so they will be able to direct any business enterprise. A copy of a letter has been seen which asks permission to put an officer trainee in an industrial firm for one week. The letter to the industrial firm said that since the

> Castro government is able to train officers only in theoretical business principles "we would appreciate it if you would take into your firm one officer for approximately one week in order *to become familiar with all phases of the business and industrial administration.*" (Italics supplied.)

This story reminds me of the young lady who, when entering the golf club one afternoon, met a friend coming out. "What have you been doing?" she said. The reply was, "Learning to play golf." The questioner then replied, "Isn't that nice! I learned yesterday."

The fact that anyone could believe a business can be mastered and business administration learned in one week is incredible. It would have been almost as absurd if the article had said one year instead of one week.

Within recent years, the Congress of the United States has made it permissible for Federal agencies to spend up to one per cent of their total budgets on manager training. Since that time there has been considerable activity toward the development of courses for training government managers. The government people have been most insistent about keeping the time required down to a minimum. Responsible representatives have requested a maximum of two weeks; one week, if possible.

There are other evidences of lack of perspective about manager training. There are those who are attracting attention by being extremely critical of something that has now become popular. Often these critics do not know what they are criticizing and the nature of their observations indicates the superficiality of their knowledge.

A prominent industrialist, who evidently is quite cynical about the development of professional management and who has little use for modern-day manager training techniques, made the following anonymous statement in a recently published book: "It's 60 per cent stuff I already knew or could have figured out, 30 per cent sheer baloney, and 10 per cent usable new knowledge." This statement indicates just a teasing amount of information and a lack of perspective on a vast subject.

Let us see if we can get this matter of manager training into proper perspective. While this presentation is necessarily limited, it is based on a broad view that an individual cannot be exposed to management for one week or one year or be sent to a management course of one, four, or thirteen weeks and end up a skilled professional manager.

There are two vast areas of knowledge a manager must master: (1) the nature of the business he is managing; (2) the principles and techniques required to manage.

Let me ask a question. How long do you think it would take an individual to learn the oil business, the telephone business, the power and light business, the automobile business, the electronics, food, or clothing business? How much do you think anyone would learn in one week about any of these industries, no matter how intensively he studied it?

It has been said that "he who can manage can manage anything." While I am probably one of the strongest believers in this philosophy, I feel that it, too, must be put in its proper perspective. In the first place, it is truer in top management than in first-line management—and it varies in acceptability between these levels. The farther removed a manager is from the actual operations of a business, the less he has to know about them. The closer he is to the supervision of the operations, the more he has to know. No professional manager, however, under any conditions, can go into any business and manage it without learning something about it.

Don G. Mitchell, former president of General Telephone and Electronics, has said that when a manager moves from one kind of a business to another, the first thing he has to do is learn the vocabulary of the new business. Well, you can't learn the vocabulary without learning a great deal about the business itself, and you can't do that in one week.

Next, let us take a look at what the manager must know about management principles and techniques.

First, he must know how to do long-range planning. Mastery of this subject requires that he understand the following: how to forecast; how to set clear-cut, attainable objectives; how to formulate courses of action; how to determine the performance that is required to attain the objectives and how to get this performance standard understood and accepted by all; how to define and appraise the factors of performance; and how to set up measurements to determine whether the desired performance is being maintained. Just how long do you think it would take a manager to become knowledgeable and skilled in this area of activity?

Secondly, the manager must know organizing. This means he must be able to arrange and relate physical and human resources required to attain his goals. He must be able to determine specifically the resources required and make provision for their proper assembly. Few things will break a manager's back quicker than inadequate or surplus inventories of things or people. Make your own estimate on how long it would take a man to conquer this subject and become skilled in it.

To be a good organizer, a man must understand the different types of organization structure: line and staff versus functional; single unit and multiple unit; single channel and multiple channel; etc. He should be adept at the use of position specifications, position descriptions, organization charts, and activity analyses.

A third area of management competency is known as executing or carrying out the plan to attain established objectives. This means that the executive must be sure that the decision to act can be made at the appropriate spot and time and with adequate authority. He must see that the decision and plan have been communicated to those responsible for taking action and that both are understood and accepted by them.

Resources must be properly assembled, arranged, and related at a predetermined time and place in accordance with the plan, and they must be prepared, tested, and ready to perform at the planned time and place. Action must be taken on schedule.

The manager who is learning how to execute the work to be done must have ways of comparing actual results with expected performance. Results must be available to him soon enough to institute corrective action, and must provide clear indication of variations from expected results. Analysis has to be made of reasons for the variations and corrective action determined.

How long do you think it will take an individual to master these skills and to understand the principles behind their use? Believe me, this is no job for an amateur, and there is no justification for oversimplifying it.

In this discussion we have dealt with only three of the major skills of a professional manager: planning, organizing, and executing. There are, as you know, still others, but any further discussion would just be driving the point into the ground.

Manager training cannot be thought of in terms of weeks or years, or in terms of specific courses or events. It is a carefully planned, directed program requiring years of experience and guidance with measured and carefully programed help.

Manager training must be thought of in these terms: basic training, internship, individual practice, current developments, and research. *Basic training* involves those years dedicated to learning the business and the principles and techniques of professional management. This stage corresponds to the years the doctor spends in school. *Internship* is practice under skilled guidance, and no manager should ever be given his first management responsibility without close, expert, daily supervision.

Individual practice gives a manager a chance to be on his own with full responsibility as a qualified professional executive who knows not only the business but also the way to manage it. *Current development* means that the modern manager must always keep up to date on the latest developments in his industry and in management practices. No man learns for all time. No manager is ever completely educated any more than any doctor is.

Research covers that activity by which the manager devotes some of his time, either within his own job or company or through some outside organization, to the discovery and validation of new principles, practices, and developments.

Manager training is a life-long proposition. The difference between today and yesterday is that today we are conscious of it; we plan it and evaluate it; we estimate the effectiveness of it in the practice of individuals who have received it. Yesterday this was all left to chance; it was a hit-or-miss proposition. It was not known what managers should know nor was there an organized attempt to see that they were taught. They learned through exposure, and their know-how was a great mass of unrelated, unorganized information.

Let there be no question about the success of managers up to this time. Those who have done well without specific, organized, and conscious manager training have done so because few others were any different and circumstances did not require more than what they had to give. The situation is different today. It is only a matter of years before the manager who has left his training to chance will be in the minority. His chances of success, therefore, will be far less than they have been in the past. I think it is well accepted that the requirements of the management job are more complex today than ever before.

There is no manager of the past who ever had problems of the same magnitude or that offered the challenge managers of today and tomorrow have to face. In view of this challenge let us put manager training—what it is and what it is all about—into proper perspective!

PART EIGHT

Changing Concepts in a Changing World

There is no greater disloyalty to the great pioneers of human progress than to refuse to budge an inch from where they stood.

DEAN W. R. INGE
Marchant: *Wit and Wisdom of Dean Inge*

"Operator, Please!"

DURING THREE DECADES OF BUSINESS EXPERIENCE, I have heard much about the need for creativity. Formal organization is frequently criticized for stifling creativity. Many studies have been made as to how you identify creativity in people. Companies go to all lengths to find creative employees. Many have special scouts for this purpose. There is a constant hue and cry for fostering an individual producer whose mind seems unlimited in its possibilities, for excusing his non-conformity, and for catering to his temperament and eccentricities.

All of this is good! We must have creativity! It could be, however, that we have the current emphasis in the wrong place. It would appear from time to time that there are more creative people than there are competent operators to make use of what has been created. There is increasing evidence of a great lack of day-to-day operating executives *who can get things done*.

Each day brings us an increasing number of illustrations of careless and poor workmanship, of incomplete staff work, of failure to meet schedules, of lack of adequate controls. There is increasing indifference on the part of production workers toward excellence—excellence in terms of quantity, quality, cost, and time.

Possibly the great search for creativity has befogged the need for productivity, and the latter has suffered. It could be that we have not kept the two in balance. If I were to identify any great need today, it would be for operators as well as creators—for people who can apply and use what has been created.

The modern executive suffers many frustrations. One of the greatest, however, is his inability to develop or secure managers at all levels who can be relied upon to get sufficient work done properly, to keep up with the potential of top management. Most organizations today have more capacity for growth than they have people to make such growth possible.

The "explosions" of the past two decades, which exceed anything in recorded history, have created and necessitated a growth which has bypassed many previously competent executives. You can see it, almost like a speedboat overtaking a sailboat. Many long-service operating executives reach a certain point in their growth and stop dead, as though they had hit the top of an elevator shaft.

Never before has so much been created in two decades as in the 1940's and 1950's. The sixties will see more than the forties and fifties combined—scientific discovery, speed at which humans can travel, explosive power, communication time, to mention a few! Consider medical progress in relation to its availability to the people of the world. It's staggering!

Civilization is hanging by its fingernails in attempting to save the world from the nuclear destruction *one* man could cause. Man will be on the moon before he knows what to do when he gets there. Housewives will have little housework to do before they know what to do with the time thus made available.

Yes, thank God for all the creativeness, but pray God to give us those who know what to do with it! Creativeness challenges the mind while productiveness challenges the soul. We have plenty of evidence that America took every precaution before risking a human life in a satellite. There are rumors and doubts as to whether the Russians did.

Let us encourage and foster creativeness with increasing determination, and let us step up, speed up, and support all intelligent effort to develop operators who can guide creativeness toward the benefit of humanity. Give me the operator who can recognize the "new" and effectively utilize it to replace the old.

Invention civilization welcomes. Application of inventions to the enhancement of human values civilization demands.

A Major Breakthrough

IT WOULD APPEAR THAT THERE MAY BE A major breakthrough in the philosophy of management people concerning the appraisal of those who work for them. While it is not a new concept or philosophy, it seems to be gaining momentum with accelerating speed.

Within my own experience, personnel appraisal is the only management activity about which there is such general agreement that it should take place, and in connection with which there is so much confusion, error, disappointment, and disillusionment. When something should be done, and when there is continuing difficulty in doing it, we should turn our attention to its basic objectives and philosophy.

What is now called appraisal used to be called rating. We drew away from the word "rating" because people did not like to be rated and they did not like the idea of being stacked up against each other by some kind of mathematical or alphabetical symbol. The word "appraisal" does not seem to be very much more acceptable. "Progress review" is now coming into more common use.

For many, many years appraisal was primarily of the personal qualities and characteristics of an individual. There might have been eight, ten, or twenty such as appearance, knowledge, intelligence, character, loyalty, dependability, and industry. In this long list an item called "performance" was sometimes included. Our perspective has grown, however, and there are now two major factors upon which people are appraised: One is performance; the other is personal qualifications. We are also getting more sensible by discussing performance first and qualifications only when they affect performance.

We still have difficulty, however. It takes considerable and unusual skill for an executive to discuss with another executive who works for him (or even for a manager to discuss with a non-supervisory employee), frankly and courageously, how well that person is doing and how well he, as an individual, fits into the over-all picture. I know of no more difficult task than for a person to be able to do this and still maintain the confidence and respect of the person with whom he is talking. Some people have a natural gift for it, but it is very rare.

One of the great difficulties with appraisal work has been the approach to it. There has been an attempt to discover weaknesses rather than opportunities for improvement. There have been evidences here and there of a desire on the part of certain people to "get something on somebody else" or to delve into the weaknesses of another. There is some kind of self-satisfaction that comes out of this, I suppose, because we may have a source of gratification in discovering others have the same or more weaknesses than we do. The difficulty encountered here is bringing truths out into the open which an individual has considered as his own personal business and has often misled himself into believing were his own secrets.

The "breakthrough" we are discussing here lies in the philosophy toward appraisal work. This philosophy, in short, is that management is *not* interested in discovering weaknesses or faults in people but *is* interested in their ultimate performance. If weaknesses can be discovered by the individual, either by himself or with the help of others, and be corrected so that performance is improved, then there is no particular reason for the manager to know what the weaknesses were or even that they existed. The whole emphasis here is upon performance and helpfulness.

Where this philosophy prevails, the management says to its people: "Annual physical examinations are highly desirable. We would like very much to have each person take them either from a doctor he chooses or from one that the company makes available. That's entirely up to the employee. The findings of the examination are discussed solely between the employee and the doctor. If, as a result, health is maintained or illness is corrected and job performance reflects nothing but good health, then the management is not interested in the physical condition or physical defects of the individual." This is purely a matter between the individual and his physician unless there is something so serious that the employee should bring it to management's attention.

The same approach applies to psychological testing. One of the great objections to psychological tests is having those for whom you work know their outcome. In some places tests are made available to people in the organization to take if they wish; counsel from a psychologist also is available. Any difficulties that show up are handled by the psychologist and the person who took the tests or received the counsel, and nothing needs to go beyond them unless there is something about which the specialist and employee feel management must be informed. Otherwise, the boss does not receive the results of the test; he is not interested in them. His interest is in the impact of this kind of service upon the performance of the employee. If performance is acceptable or improved, the employee's problems are nobody's business but his own and the psychologist's.

There are companies that provide experienced counseling service to employees on any problems they want to discuss. These counselors talk with the employees, give them advice, and in many instances do nothing more than give them a shoulder to cry on. What is exposed in such situations does not go beyond the employee or the counselor, but the employee's performance usually improves as a result. Again, let us repeat the philosophy: Management is not interested in finding out the defects in a particular situation if some assistance can be rendered to correct them so that performance is improved.

In other words, the breakthrough is the philosophy that management provides help without knowing what help or whether the help is needed. If the person involved feels justified in accepting this help, then its outcome is up to the employee to divulge to the extent he wishes. The employer's final interest is in the performance of the person.

This means that appraisal work is restricted to actual performance as evaluated in terms of results and methods. The personal relationships, difficulties, characteristics, qualifications become matters between specialists and the employee. This, therefore, leaves personal situations in the hands of skilled people and removes from management the embarrassment of discussing personal shortcomings with individuals. The boss is now in a position to work constructively at helping the person do a better job and look for opportunities for improvement.

"Do Gooders" and "Good Doers"

PERHAPS IT IS BECAUSE I HAVE DEVOTED MUCH of my own life to trying to help improve human welfare that I have become disturbed about the way a concentrated interest in "doing good" frequently results in a distorted view of the general character of human beings.

There are more people in this world who are doing well than there are people in trouble. "Do gooders" are dealing all the time in statistics that indicate trouble. Because of this concentration on problem cases, they frequently develop the impression that trouble is the pattern of the world. There is a tendency for many "do gooders" to develop an intensity that negates their original dedication to a noble cause. Presumably motivated by a desire to work for human welfare, they regard humans as statistics. An individual becomes Case #3281 B.

Sometimes, in an effort to build up the importance of a cause and to make certain human problems big enough to justify great expenditures of time and money, statistics become padded and slightly overdone.

A baby, used once for a scene in a Hollywood movie, thereafter may be identified as an unemployed person eligible for unemployment benefits. A compensation case may be continued far beyond any reasonable period based on the actual condition of the claimant. (It is possible that compensation added to income from personal insurance may exceed income from work.)

Many "do gooders" really believe—and make others believe—that the world is all wrong and that a great majority of the human beings in it have been wronged. Actually, there are millions of "good doers" who are well adjusted in life. They understand their responsibilities and obligations; they have jobs and are happy in them; they are married and have fine families; they attend and participate in local church and community affairs. They are fine, all-around citizens. They have no particular problems requiring help from others and they are fulfilling their obligations. There are no statistics on such people; there is no intense interest in them. They are taking care of themselves and making their contribution in their own way. These are the people that really make the world tick.

In the early 1930's, it was my privilege to appear for the first time on a program of the Industrial Conference at Silver Bay on Lake George, New York. What I had to say I said with considerable conviction and feeling. There was no doubt in my mind that if everyone followed my suggestions, we would reach the millennium within twenty-four hours, or forty-eight hours at the outside.

In the audience was a dear old gentleman named Sam Graflin, a retired executive of the Ward Baking Company. After the meeting he took me by the arm and led me outside to a bench under a huge maple tree. We chatted for a while about the subject matter of my talk. Then he said something I have never forgotten: "You know, Appley, there were a lot of fine people in this world before you were born, and they did much for civilization. There are still a lot of fine people to be born, and for heaven's sake leave something for them to do!"

There are several lessons in this statement by Sam Graflin. The first is that there have been, and are, and are going to be, many fine people in this world—"good doers." A second lesson is that people on the whole have made constructive contributions to mankind that far outweigh contributions to human misery. A third lesson is that we should not let our intense concern over what is wrong in the world blind us to the fact that everything cannot be corrected within the span of one generation. Each of us should strive to make his own little contribution to better the lives of others.

There are people who are physically or mentally ill; there are people who are unemployed; there are intolerable working conditions and work relationships; there is juvenile delinquency; there are alcoholics and dope addicts. All of them deserve and require dedicated attention and practical assistance. In the process, however, of alleviating such conditions, let us not lose sight of the fact that great segments of humanity are doing well under good conditions, and that the proportion of the population that they represent is increasing with each generation.

In the midst of all the condemnation of what is bad in the world, a little commendation for and recognition of those who are good can be inspiring and helpful. It may be well to point out to the "do gooders" that the unfortunates with whom they work are human beings with flesh and blood, hearts and souls, and not just case numbers. It also may be well for "do gooders" to realize that the world is not as bad as it looks when one takes only statistics into account, and that there are a lot of "good doers" who make the world, with all its difficulties, a pretty nice place in which to live.

If one is vitally interested in slum clearance and as a result spends much time in the slums, he should remember that the slum area represents about five per cent of what otherwise is a fine, clean, and progressive city. If one is trying to reduce juvenile delinquency and, therefore, spends a great deal of time with delinquents, a special effort must be made to realize that a very small percentage of juveniles are delinquents. In other words, let us be sure that the time and effort spent in one area of human need do not color our thinking to such an extent that we lose our perspective about the world in which we live.

Managers Must Be Dynamic

MOST PEOPLE SEEM TO BE CREATURES OF habit. Once they have become accustomed to an environment or practice, they are irritated by any change.

Every commuter is familiar with those who stand at the same spot on the platform every morning, sit in the same seat on the train, read the newspaper in exactly the same way, stand up in the aisle at the same moment before the train arrives at its destination, and follow the same route to the subway.

We are all aware how we get into certain routines in our homes. Certain chairs become known as Dad's chair and Mother's chair. In due time they become worn and battered, but any replacement of them or even of the upholstery irks us until we have adjusted ourselves to the new situation.

Workers become accustomed to old factories and old offices. For months after a move there are constant complaints and a continuing stream of grievances about conditions that are still unfamiliar, even though the new quarters may be objectively much more desirable.

A foreman who replaces an unpopular one often is

as unpopular as his predecessor, at least at first, for the workers were used to the old boss with all his eccentricities and the new one is an unknown quantity.

Human though all this may be, managers cannot permit themselves to become victims of habit or tradition, the past or the present. Managers must think constantly in terms of change. They must be consciously seeing to it that things are different and that old customs are replaced by new ones, that new goals make old ones look small, that new ideas make present ones inadequate.

Life is dynamic; society is dynamic; managers, therefore, must be dynamic if they are to keep pace with the conditions about them. When a manager or management becomes satisfied with what is, reluctant to accept change, smug and complacent about success to date, that manager or management is dead though still breathing.

I have had the privilege of observing two managers in action in situations that illustrate this point. The first is the president of a small, well-established company with products that are required and in demand; in its ten-year history this business has reached an annual volume of $2.5 million.

I listened to this president as he presented to his officers a pie chart representing the total volume of sales of products the company is now manufacturing and distributing and the probable volume of sales of related products the company has every right to believe it should manufacture and distribute. The chart showed the proportion of business the company now enjoys and the proportion of business it might enjoy in other products within ten years if it went into the manufacture of those products. The president then mapped out a program, which had been developed with the full participation of those present as well as with the aid of outside experts, indicating that in ten years the company should be doing a $35-million business. My guess is that it will be.

The other experience was of a large company, about 60 years old, doing a business of more than $700 million. This, again, was a meeting of the company's top executives, at which the president presented a program indicating that in the next five years the firm's business would more than double, requiring the addition to the payroll of more than 40,000 persons. There is no question in my mind, knowing these executives, that this will be accomplished.

The changes that will have to take place in those two companies, if these new objectives are to be attained, are almost impossible to conceive. We know there will be changes in products, facilities, personnel, organization structure—all of which add up to continuing changes in working habits and relationships.

A manager would laugh if you asked him to work today under the conditions and with the facilities of 30 or 40 years ago. *But the conditions and facilities with which he is working today will be just as laughable 30 years from now.*

The manager of tomorrow may have one whole office

wall in the form of a wide-angle screen onto which he can bring for a conference executives from all over the country or the world. On the desk in front of him he may have a small screen to which he can bring, even from the other side of the earth, an individual with whom he wishes to talk.

The manager of tomorrow may have in his pocket a gadget no bigger than a cigarette case through which he can dictate at will to some central point, where his message will be transcribed and back in his hands within a matter of seconds. In his office he may have a machine to which he can dictate and in no time at all receive as many copies as he wishes. From his office he may step directly onto a parking roof, get into a taxicopter, and take off for any point he wishes.

Most important, the manager of tomorrow will have available to him pertinent facts in sufficient volume quickly enough to make highly important decisions in a matter of seconds. The information that the manager has today is skimpy compared with the information that will be available to him in the next few years.

The world is dynamic. It may suffer slight temporary slumps, reflecting human frailty, but the continuing trend is ahead to growth and progress. Growth and progress require changes in human environment, in human habits. The manager must be the kind of person who can visualize these changes, make them easily, adapt himself to them, and make them work for the good of the human beings who make up the organization he is leading.

Very little that we had or used a quarter of a century ago is adequate for today's conditions and challenges. Very little that we have today will be of use tomorrow. We have only to think of electronics and atomic energy to know that the next half-century will make the past half-century look like playing in a sandbox.

Managers must be optimistic about the future. They must provide and plan for stupendous growth. Managers must know that change is inevitable. They must be intelligent and competent in controlling the nature and rate of the growth. Managers cannot be creatures of habit, allergic to change. Managers at all levels must be dynamic.

Research vs. Gimmicks

FREQUENTLY, SOME CHIEF EXECUTIVE IS heard to say, "My only problem is people." Actually, this is more factual than facetious. One of the reasons that people are a problem is that people do not understand people.

Hardly a day goes by that the world is not startled by some completely unexpected action by an individual or a group of individuals. There probably is no greater problem, for whose solution executives are hunting gimmicks, than those in human motivation. There is a superficial search for some patent package that will help us solve the most serious and most challenging problem in the world today.

It is common practice for management to employ expert help and spend considerable time and money on problems in product lines, product processes, distribution methods, financial structure, and all kinds of systems and procedures. The amount of money and time spent on human research, however, is practically negligible by comparison.

At a recent meeting of twenty-five corporation presidents we were discussing questions such as these: How can we get people to think constructively and broadly about the company, particularly at the management level? How can a president set up objectives and goals, as well as long-range plans, that are sufficiently challenging to call for the best effort from all management echelons? How can managers get unionized employees to realize that their own effectiveness in job performance has a direct relationship to the perpetuation of the business that makes their jobs available?

These are important questions for any company and management. If products, finance, and processes require research and engineering, certainly human motivations need more. Since it is such an important problem, it would seem reasonable that one of the first steps managements should take is to set up specific budgets and facilities, as well as personnel, to study these situations in their own companies. The more companies that participate in such work, the more these studies could be combined in over-all research for industry and business as a whole.

There are some companies in this country that have been doing this sort of thing for a long time and have been in very close relationship with some of our universities and the work they are doing. It is encouraging to note the increasing interest in specific research along these lines and the indication that more and more companies will be getting into it in the not too distant future.

Some of the findings resulting from the significant

research in human motivations that has been done would make management a lot easier if they were more broadly known. Any serious attempt, therefore, to find the answers to some of the questions that have been stated here should consist, first, of finding out what has been done and what is available now; and, second, of a specific and concerted effort to contribute to further findings in this area.

No research is required to find gimmicks that will improve human relationships. The time, effort, and money expended in the search for such gimmicks, therefore, would be much more productive were they put into actual research on the problems themselves.

For the People

DURING ITS FORMALIZATION AND DEVELOPMENT over the past half-century, the personnel function in American business and industry has been faced with numerous challenges and has met them all reasonably effectively. World War I raised to an emergency peak the need for training and "rating." The depression of the 1930's brought the challenge of government regulation and supervision in close collaboration with the rapid and successful development of organized labor. World War II produced a crisis in the nature of a manpower shortage in war production plants which had to be met by voluntary means. Since World War II, the gaps in management ranks left by the recession and the war have called for blitzkrieg methods of executive development.

The personnel administration function is, during the next decade, faced with a challenge that far exceeds all those just cited. In fact, the crises of the past fifty years fade into obscurity when an analysis is made of what lies ahead.

Brand-new relationships now exist between organized labor and the Federal Government, and the Administration seems to sense the deep responsibility and obligation resulting therefrom. Without the slightest indication of the import of it all, one must observe that this must be followed closely and understood adequately.

There is new management know-how on the part of top executives in today's business and industry. The "old guard"—who came up the hard way, wore the overalls into the front office, and knew all the answers to everything—is now gone. Even those oldsters who were held over in management ranks during the management shortages of the war and the postwar era are gone. Today's managers are either skilled in, or conscious of, professional management as a concept and a practice. They understand human motivations as their predecessors never did and, to some degree, are skilled in personnel administration. Many of them were trained in this field of specialization.

Foreign operations by American companies are a foregone conclusion. It is my impression that there is no human being alive today who knows and comprehends the full extent of this activity as it now exists, or the rapidity with which it will grow. Big business is going and must continue to go abroad for markets, lower costs, and better quality. Small business is going and must continue to go abroad, if it is to go anywhere, because of the unfavorable results of the administration of current inheritance taxes and anti-trust laws in this country.

This means that American management is moving

rapidly in its search for knowledge of how to compete abroad. Business men are also searching for a means by which they can explain to their people in this country why they have to do this.

And so we could go on with increasing factors of the "new look" during the next ten years. The purpose of this presentation, however, is to make one point. In view of the nature of the inevitable challenges and crises of the 1960's (and many more of them might be cited than are referred to here), the function of personnel administration must direct its attention toward the development of philosophies, ethics, skills, and media which will put *American business and industry on the side of the people.* Highly skilled, organized, dedicated, and financed pressure groups have been reasonably successful in placing business and industry on the defense in this regard.

Individual companies must become identified with community interests. They cannot avoid responsibility for solving unemployment problems. Neither can they solve them individually. They must join with, lead, and become identified with community effort toward this end.

Business leadership cannot be indifferent to the rapidly increasing medical costs in our society today. This cannot be handled individually. We get nowhere by fighting socialized medicine when current practices are driving the people right in that direction. Business and industry must become collectively identified with the solution of this problem.

Housing is not just a government problem. Substandard housing is as much a responsibility of the business and industrial community as it is of the social community. Business, as such, must become identified with programs to improve housing and living conditions.

Transportation is a community problem. No one is affected by it more than business and industry. Business and industrial leaders must, therefore, become involved in the leadership and organization of community effort to solve what is now driving groups of citizens into panic. Jobs and homes are being threatened.

There have been many references to business in politics. This activity is gaining much attention and support. Without expressing any opinion on the matter, I would like to state the belief that such problems as I have cited here could be kept out of politics if business and industrial leaders accepted their rightful responsibilities within the communities in which they operate. "Community" is used in its broadest sense.

This all means that the personnel function must represent expertness in communication, organization, and leadership. It must deliberately and effectively place business and industry in its rightful, helpful place in the minds and hearts of the people, as well as in their lives.

A Colossal Paradox

A VERY ABLE, INTELLIGENT, WELL-EDUCATED, and professionally successful young man in his early thirties recently asked me, "Why is it the American business man has failed so miserably in identifying himself as a friend of the worker?"

That is a profound question. The business man (and within this general term we include the producer, the manufacturer, and the merchant) is one who creates and maintains jobs, who meets payrolls, who provides financial and non-financial benefits and incentives, who has most to do with the maintenance and improvement of the standard of living of the American worker. Yet he is often thought of as anti-worker. Witness a phrase used commonly today—"management versus labor."

How can this be? Why is it so? Who has a clear-cut, generally acceptable answer? Although I do not know the answer, let me suggest a possible one for the sake of discussion.

The business man carries heavy responsibility. He must operate, direct, and actually be engaged in the functioning of an organization that can produce products and/or services of a quality and at a cost that will create sufficient income to pay wages and incentives to workers, a fair return to stockholders, taxes to the government, and still have enough to plow back into the business to insure its perpetuation. All this has to be done within the framework of rigid laws, regulations, ethics, and human standards.

This is a full-time job. It takes a lot of skill, a lot of training, a lot of dedication, a lot of time. If he succeeds, greater successes are expected of him. If he fails, he must take sole responsibility for the consequences. In the performance of his task, the business man is held accountable. He can be openly accused, indicted, convicted, fined, and put in jail. He must act and speak with caution and discretion.

The business man is a busy man providing for the welfare of hundreds and thousands of people. He is producing that which others enjoy. He does not have the time, the inclination, or the skill to sell or defend himself other than through his performance on the job.

Over against this, there are individuals and groups that sustain and perpetuate themselves as full-time advocates of "what's good for the people." They do not build jobs; they do not maintain jobs; they do not meet payrolls or pay dividends; they pay only personal income taxes that they cannot avoid. They have nothing to do but to sell themselves and their causes to the people and to build themselves up as the exclusive benefactors of the people by tearing down the real benefactors. These people usually are sustained by the contributions of those who think they are better off because of the activities of such representatives. It does not seem to occur to those who support the self-publicized benefactor that he produces nothing. He consumes only, and he spends his time needling and discrediting those who do produce.

In other words, he who produces that which is necessary for the welfare of the people has his hands full doing just that. He does not spend the time and the talent required to sell the value of his deeds. At the same time, there are people devoting all their energy and all their effort to discounting what the producer is doing.

When a business man does become impressed by this situation and takes time to leave the job and the office to sell the importance of his work, he is immediately suspect. What he says is popularly discounted because he is "pro-business," "pro-management." Why is this so immediately accepted as condemnation in itself? Is there anything wrong with being pro-labor, pro-farmer, pro-educator, pro-veteran? What's the matter with being pro-business or pro-management? Is the implication that business or management should not represent itself as well as possible?

Maybe the answer lies in the fact that all selfish interest preys upon the hand that feeds it. Maybe it is because the business man is the object of attack by so many individuals and pressure groups that it is virtually impossible for him to make any headway in representing his own position.

The greatest food upon which the self-ordained "friend of the people" feasts is selfish interest. His theme is that people should get more and more for less and less. This is sure to fuel the furnace of popularity. Never in my experience, however, has a person who sings this theme ever produced anything that increased anyone's income, enlarged anyone's benefits, or increased anyone's pride in work well done.

If such an individual goes to jail, he is a martyr. It is useless to sue him because he has nothing. It is foolish to fine him because he cannot pay, or he uses the funds of others to defend himself. He cannot be held accountable because he has no responsibility. He, therefore, says what he wishes to say and makes whatever accusations he wishes to make with reckless abandon and impish delight.

It seems to me that the business man has not popularized himself as a friend of the worker because he is too busy producing what the worker needs and wants. His opposition consists of a solid phalanx of individuals and groups who live on the promise they will get more for people by shaking it loose from the producers.

Finding an answer to this problem is a challenge facing all business men today.

Profit!

ANYONE WHO HAS NOT MET A PAYROLL, PAID for materials received, paid a fair return to stockholders who have loaned their life savings to the enterprise, met a tax bill, accepted financial community obligations, set aside a reserve for perpetuation and growth of an organization, should not read any further. He cannot understand what is about to be said.

Those who criticize, urge curtailment of, and/or denounce profit, and those who campaign to distribute it without regard to contribution to it, are dependent upon profit. A welfare state can exist only in a profit economy. A welfare state never created what it distributes. Only profit, or debt, can be distributed, and unless debt is paid off from profits, bankruptcy is inevitable.

It is nothing short of alarming to hear some of the people who are sincerely questioning the profit motive in this day and age. Many individuals who are an integral part of the private enterprise system express doubt when any emphasis is placed upon or acknowledgment given to the importance of profit.

Let there be no doubt that the sole purpose of business is to make a profit! Each business and each enterprise have some product or service that consumers want or need. Success depends upon the capability of the corporation to produce that service or product at a quality and at a price the consumer will accept. When this choice is removed from the consumer, cost will inevitably increase and quality will just as certainly decrease.

No product and no service, regardless of its quality, regardless of its cost, regardless of the need or desire of the consumer, can continue to be available, however, unless the corporation that manages and distributes it makes a profit over a continuing period of time. Short-range losses are probable and, in many cases, advisable, but long-range gains are an absolute necessity.

"Profit" is an honorable and distinctive word. There are few words in the English vocabulary that have any clearer meaning or significance. The making of profit is an honorable and desirable objective. Those who have not been so engaged, so motivated, and successful at it, however, do not have any real understanding of it. It is, furthermore, absolutely impossible for any human being who has not faced bankruptcy and failure because of the lack of profit to comprehend the significance of it with anywhere near the same depth as one who has.

May I plead for at least two reactions by human beings in the United States of America: First, mentally accept the rightness and the necessity of profit as the very essence of the private enterprise system which is the economic backbone of this country. Second, when you read or listen to someone expound on the subject of profit, or profit making, please find out his or her qualifications to do so. If such a person has not made or lost profit, do not listen to him—he doesn't know anything about it!

A further plea is directed toward an understanding that profit can be made by unfair and crooked means. Profit can be used for undesirable or criminal ends. This, however, is the essence of democracy: Right and wrong are permitted within a democracy, but wrong ultimately brings to bear upon itself the vengeance of the people. Let us not condemn something that is good because it may be subject to evil intent.

I believe in profit. I believe the world is better for it. I believe those who can make it honorably and distribute it justly are to be commended and revered, and those who use it to exploit people and manipulate funds should be punished with all the vehemence at the command of an outraged public. I do not believe that any single segment of society—religion, education, government, business, labor, agriculture, or personal service—is in any position to stand in judgment of the others. Honor and guilt are to be found in all these segments. What is important is the belief and practice of the individual. This is democracy! This is freedom! This is the very essence of the basic plan of civilization, which, I firmly believe, is controlled by a greater Power than mankind.

The Past Is Prologue

IT IS NOT AT ALL UNCOMMON TO READ OR HEAR a statement such as "There are two kinds of people in the world" or "People can be divided into three classifications." The fact of the matter is, of course, that people can be divided into many different kinds of categories, depending upon the particular area of human activity being discussed.

Although conscious of the triteness of such phraseology, I venture to start out by saying that, in terms of accomplishments, managers can be grouped into two broad categories: those who are pleased with and influenced by the accomplishments of the past and those who are primarily occupied with the future.

Many managers are more impressed with the effort they have expended on the job and how much they have accomplished than they are with the problem of how to do more with less effort. They do not realize that the past is of value only as an introduction to the future.

It is reassuring to see the tremendous increase these days in that management activity known as long-range planning. There is much discussion of it; there is extensive research into the techniques of it; there are many tangible programs resulting from it; and there is great evidence that it pays off.

Some managers, however, seem to have a mental block against long-range planning. They say that you cannot see "that far ahead." To them, the future is so uncertain and the conditions under which they are going to be operating are so completely unknown that it is hard for them to see how they can plan.

This type of concern results from a lack of understanding of the impact of planning. When plans are made for a long time ahead, more is accomplished than would have been attained without them. Even though a plan is missed by "one hundred miles," there is a net gain. A psychology of waiting for future developments is changed to one of trying to determine future developments. It is "a plan" that is important and not certainty.

Recently I have participated in several discussions dealing with the economic conditions under which we now live and those that we might anticipate. On many of these occasions I have heard it said that the extensiveness of long-range planning is a new factor in the economy and is having much to do with the rapidity with which we come out of temporary lulls and slumps. It seems to be quite evident that when men are thinking of the future they get the present into its proper perspective. Immediate difficulties are handled with greater dispatch in the midst of an attitude of impatience with anything which interferes with the long-range goals.

It is not difficult to spot those who are more proud of the past than concerned with the future. It is easy, too, to spot things that have been done the same way for decades. The prime illustration of this is in the area of marketing. In company after company one can find nothing new in marketing plans, sales techniques, and salesmen's activities. The slightest bit of research into what improvements have taken place in selling startles one out of any complacency about our nation's capacity to sell its way out of difficulties.

No particular case, of course, can be built for changing just for the sake of change. However, it is reasonable to suspect, at least until investigation proves otherwise, that in a rapidly changing economy and society such as ours a lack of change in approach may indicate complacency. If there is nothing radically new or different about the way we are doing old jobs, the chances are that we have fallen asleep at the switch.

We are inclined to assume that certain conditions are true just because they seem always to have been so. Sensitivity to changing consumer interest and demand is an essential ingredient in any company. It is good from time to time to spend money, lots of money, in investigating whether the methods we have used in the past are still adequate to meet the goals of the future.